Bernard Homer Dixon

The Border or Riding Clans

Followed by a History of the Clan Dickson and a brief Account of the Family of the

Author

Bernard Homer Dixon

The Border or Riding Clans
Followed by a History of the Clan Dickson and a brief Account of the Family of the Author

ISBN/EAN: 9783337250188

Printed in Europe, USA, Canada, Australia, Japan

Cover: Foto ©Suzi / pixelio.de

More available books at **www.hansebooks.com**

THE

Border or Riding Clans

FOLLOWED BY A HISTORY

OF THE

CLAN DICKSON

AND

A BRIEF ACCOUNT OF THE FAMILY OF THE AUTHOR,

B. HOMER DIXON, K. N. L.

———————

PRINTED ORIGINALLY FOR PRESENTATION ONLY AND NOW ENLARGED.

———————

ALBANY, N. Y.:
JOEL MUNSELL'S SONS, PUBLISHERS.
1889.

CONTENTS.

NOTE.

The first edition of this little work was privately printed for the writer's own family and friends only, but as several applications were made for copies this enlarged edition has been placed in the publisher's hands.

Not having been originally intended for publication several extracts were made without preserving the names of the authorities, which the general reader will not require, but, as the dates have been generally given, the critical reader will find no difficulty in verifying my statements.

THE BORDER CLANS.

By the word "clans" is generally if not almost universally understood those of the Scottish Highlands, few being aware how important a part our clans played during the Middle Ages, and I trust, therefore, this little treatise concerning the Border, Riding or Foraying clans, Dalesmen, Marchmen or Borderers, as they were variously styled, may not prove uninteresting, as they have too long been viewed through nineteenth century spectacles, and have, moreover, been generally confounded with the Batablers or Baitablers, as the English called them, or freebooters of the Debateable Lands,* whose hands were against every man and every man's hands were against them. These frontier rievers, who in Scottish legal documents were generally called bordour men or broken men, acquired also about the time of James the First (1406–1437) the name of Mosstroopers, from their living in the mosses of the country.

Previous to the union of the crowns in 1603, the borders and the highlands were in a state totally

* In a document of A. D. 1588, these are styled "sumtyme callit Debettable."

different from the rest of Scotland and were subjected
to laws different from the remainder of the kingdom.
The feudal system, which formed the principal ground-
work of ancient law, both civil and criminal, had in
those districts a comparatively imperfect influence.
The inhabitants were divided into surnames or clans,
who acknowledged no supremacy saving that of their
chief, chieftain or head of their name, who might
often be a person entirely different from their feudal
superior or over-lord as he was called in Scottish law.

The border clans have usually been considered as
little better than common thieves, none apparently
reflecting that the actual state of both England and
Scotland was with brief exemptions one of chronic
petty warfare, nor upon the general state of society
in those days when the Bible and other books were
almost unknown, for the first printing press in London was only set up in 1476, and printing was not
introduced into Scotland until 1501.

Copies of the English Bible found their way into
Scotland, however, and were of great service in pro-
moting and establishing the reformed doctrines, and
in 1543, four years before Cranmer's Reformation
was completed in England, Lord Robert Maxwell
submitted to parliament a bill making it lawful for
all " our Soverane Ladyis lieges to possess and read
copies of the Bible in Scotch or English." It was of
course opposed by the bishops, but was nevertheless
sanctioned by parliament, and some years after a
license to print " ye Inglis Bybill " was granted in

1568, but the translation was not issued until 1579, when it was enacted by parliament that each householder worth three hundred marks of yearly rent and all substanteous yeomen and burgesses esteemed as worth five hundred pounds in land and goods should have a Bible and psalm-book in the vulgar tongue under the penalty of ten pounds.

Manuscript newsletters were ushered in in London in the fifteenth century, followed in the next century by the printed news book. These, however, were but little known beyond the large cities, and the first newspaper did not appear in England until after the union and in Scotland until the Caledonian Mercury was issued in 1660.

William Barlow, Bishop of St. Asaph's, English Ambassador in Scotland, complained to Cromwell, Lord Privy Seal, of the state of the English borders, and gave a very similar apology for his own countrymen. The abstract of his letter in Thorpe's State Papers is as follows :

" Berwick, Feb. 10, 1535." " A long letter, on the miserable misorder, ruinous decay and intolerable calamity of His Grace's* subjects on the borders ; there is no knowledge of Christ's gospel, although there are plenty of priests, multitudes of monks and flocking companies of friars." †

---

*The King, Henry VIII, was then styled "His Grace."

† This letter was written one year after the English Parliament established the King as Supreme Head of the Church, thus sweeping away the papal headship.

Ignorance was so profound in the Dark Ages that even among the priests and monks, who were supposed to be educated, nearly all of them said by rote the services they had learned by heart, and it has been computed that there were not more than one or two at the outside, *in every thousand,* who were capable both of reading and writing. Of course there were exceptional cases of students fond of learning, but they were of comparatively rare occurrence. It is true there were burgh schools at Perth, Stirling and Roxburgh at a very early period, and a convent school at the latter place in the time of Malcolm IV (1153–1165), and there was a village school at Norham-on-Tweed in the twelfth century, but probably they were frequented principally by the children of the trades people, who had to keep some accounts, and but by few of them. As there were then no printed books, the education given must have been very limited.

In 1494, parliament ordained through all the realm that all barons and substantial freeholders,* put their eldest sons and heirs to the schools at the age of six, or at the utmost nine years; who are to remain at the grammar schools till they have a competent foundation and skill in Latin. After which they are to study three years in the schools of arts and laws; so that they may have knowledge in the laws, and by this means justice be distributed throughout all the realm; those who become sheriffs or judges ordinary, having proper understanding, and the poor

* Probably signifying freeholders in towns, not barons.

being under no necessity of recourse to high courts for every small injury.

This statute seems not to have extended to the lords and earls whose profession was arms and hunting alone!

In England, as Speed informs us, there were 30,000 studying in the university of Oxford alone, but Hume says "What was the occupation of these young men? To learn bad Latin and still worse logic," and that Hume was not speaking without reason is shown by Platina, librarian of the Vatican (which then contained 2,500 volumes), who died in 1481, who says of the notaries or the prothonotary of the city of Rome itself, whose office it was to commit to writing all memorable occurrences belonging to the church, "But in our age most of them (not to say all) are so ignorant that they are scarcely able to write their own names in Latin, much less to transmit the actions of others."

Even as late as the Reformation such was the want of knowledge in England that Bishop Hooper, in 1550, found one hundred and sixty-eight, or more than half of his clergy in the diocese of Gloucester, who could not repeat the ten commandments; forty who could not tell when the Lord's prayer was written and thirty-one of them ignorant who was its author!

These were priests who had just come out of the church of Rome, and the case was no better in Scotland, for only a few years previously (in 1538) the

Bishop of Dunkeld having cited Dean Forrest, Vicar of Dolour, to appear before him for the heinous crime of "preaching every Sunday to his parishoners upon the epistles and gospels of the day," he desired him to forbear "seeing his diligence that way brought him in suspicion of heresie." If he could find a *good gospel* or a *good epistle*, that made for the liberty of the holy church, the bishop willed him to preach that to his people and let the rest be. The dean replying " That he had read both the new testament and the old and that he had never found an ill epistle or an ill gospel in any of them;" the bishop said " I thank God I have lived well these many years and never knew either the old or the new. I content me with my Portuise and my Pontifical, and if you Dean Thomas leave not these fantasies you will repent when you cannot mend it."

Here we have a Roman Catholic bishop declaring in open court that he had never read the Bible and desired nothing but his breviary and book of rites and ceremonies. It is hardly necessary to add that the dean suffered martyrdom, having been burned to death.

With such a lack of education it is not surprising, therefor, to see bonds to the king given by heads of clans, promising to keep good rule or to furnish armed men or the like, often signed "with our hands at the pen led by John Andro," or " John Andro for those who cannot write."

Walter Scott of Satchells, when he dictated his

history, called himself "Captain Walter Scott, an old souldier and no scholler,

> And one that can write nane,
> But just the letters of his name."

One of the last contracts or pledges to the crown, being a general band or bond against thieves, murderers and oppressors, was made as late at 1602, and among the lairds who subscribed thereto is "Johnne Inglis of Manerheid (with my hand at the pen led by James Primrois, Clerk of the Counsale, at my command because I cannot write)," and Maxwells, Turnbulls, Kers, Scotts and others make the same confession — but nevertheless they could handle the sword and spear, and were

> "Steady of heart and stout of hand
> As ever drove prey from Cumberland."

These were Kers,* Scotts (the two great rival families), Homes, Elliots, Johnstones, Grahams, Armstrongs, Irvings, Cranstouns, Cockburns, Maxwells, Gladstones, Dicksons and others who were always ready for the fray and only counted a predatory excursion one of the ordinary diversions of everyday life — replaced in a measure in the present day by shooting tame partridges or pheasants in preserves or following the hounds. The man who plundered another's cattle would perhaps meet him soon after at a border meeting and joke and gamble and drink with him, although quite ready to fight, if necessary,

---

* This name was usually written Ker on the Scottish side and Carr on the English side.

rather than give up his spoils — except for a con-
sideration !

For notwithstanding their mutual hostilities and
reciprocal depredations a natural intercourse took
place between the English and Scottish marchers at
these meetings and during the short intervals of
peace. They met frequently also at parties of the
chace or foot-ball ; and it required many and strict
regulations to prevent them from forming intermar-
riages and from cultivating too close an intimacy.
This humanity and moderation was, however, in the
case of deadly feud entirely laid aside. Their vengeance then not only vented itself upon the homicide
and his friends but upon all his kindred and tribe.

Yet still the report of Sir Robert Bowes when he
invaded Scotland in 1545, speaks volumes. The
English borderers would not burn down the standing
corn and he had to draft Irishmen for the purpose.

The friendly meetings took place on "days of trew
(*truce*)" or "March days," * principally to settle scores
for depredations and injuries on either side, of which
there was a rough tariff, generally acknowledged as
border law, and this law made it death for an Englishman or Scotchman to draw weapon upon his greatest
foe from the time of holding the court till next morn·
ing at sunrise, it being judged that in this interval
all might return home.

One of these was held at Reidswire in the Cheviots
in 1575, which ended in one of the last of the border

---

* Not the month but the frontier.

fights. The clans of the Middle Marches with Sir John Carmichael, deputy keeper of Liddesdale, at their head, there met the English Borderers of Tynedale and Redesdale under Sir John Forster, the English warden of the Middle Marches. The meeting began as usual in mirth and good fellowship. Booths were erected, drink was sold and an impromptu fair sprung up. But while all went on merrily the two leaders quarrelled. The English took umbrage at the pretensions of the Scot, and rising in his stirrups gave a signal to his men of Tynedale who forthwith discharged a flight of arrows. Then both sides set to work with sword and spear and bended bow, and a fight ensued which was decided at last in favor of the Scots, although the English had the advantage in point of numbers.

The Scotts of Buccleugh were there with "The Laird's Wat," as Scott of Goldiland was called,* at their head.

> "The Armestranges that aye hae been a
> hardie house but not a hail,†
> The Elliots honours to maintaine brought
> down the lave‡ o' Liddesdale,
> The Sheriffe brought the Douglas down
> Wi' Cranstane, Gladstain good at need,
> Beanjeddart bauldy made him boun§
> Wi' a' the Trumbills stronge and stout,
> The Rutherfoords with gret renown.
> Of other clans I cannot tell,
> Because our warning was not wide "—

---

* Some say, however, this was Walter Scott of Ancrum.
† Not hail or whole, because they were an outlawed or broken clan.
‡ Rest.   § Archibald of Bonjedburgh made himself ready.

On the English side were

> "Five hundred Fenwicks in a flock
> Wi' Sir John Foster for their guyde
> Full fifteen hundred men and mae."

Sir John Heron one of the English leaders was slain and the warden and several others taken prisoners. The queen, as might have been expected of the daughter of bluff Harry was furious when she heard how her men had been chased across the border, and the Regent Morton, to appease her, sent the Scottish leader a prisoner to England, but good Queen Bess was too magnanimous to take vengeance on a helpless foeman. The English court moreover being convinced that their own warden was in the wrong, not only discharged Carmichael with honor, but even gave him a present.

Our forefathers called this fight an unhappy accident only. In a proclamation of the regent warning the people not to take advantage of it, and to keep the peace, it is styled the "unhappy accident at the lait meeting on the Reid Swyre."

It must be remembered that although when the English invaded us reprisals followed as a matter of course, still it was not in private forays only that our Marchmen were engaged. They acted as a sort of border militia to protect their country not only from the English but also from the baitablers, and frequently bound themselves to the king to that effect. In a tax levied in 1586, for a force of waged men on the border, the border shires are expressly exempted from taxation on the ground of personal service.

In 1522, the Earl of Shrewsbury invaded the king-dom, burnt part of the town of Kelso and, according to some writers, burnt eighty villages also and razed eighteen towers of stone, but he was met by the Borderers of the Merse and Teviotdale and forced to retreat with considerable loss.

In 1523, the Earl of Surrey crossed the borders with ten thousand mercenaries besides other forces, but was so annoyed by the Scotch skirmishers that he wrote to his king "I assure your grace I found the Scottes at this tyme the boldest men and the hottest that ever I sawe any nation. And all the jorney upon all parts of the armye kept us with so contynuall skyrmyshe that I never sawe the like. If they might assemble Xl^ti M^t as good men as I now sawe XV^c or ij M^t; it wold bee a herd encountre to mete theym."

Surrey's praise is valuable, being that of a good soldier who had often been employed on foreign ser-vice.

In 1532, the Earl of Northumberland detached fifteen hundred men who ravaged and plundered the lands of Sir Walter Scott of Buccleugh and burned Branksome, but failed in their principal object which was to kill or make him prisoner. In resentment for this Sir Walter and other border chiefs assembled three thousand men whom with consummate skill and valor they conducted into England, laid waste a large part of Northumberland, baffled and defeated the English and returned home laden with booty.

In August, 1542, Sir Robert Bowes with three thousand horse attempted to enter Scotland, but was defeated at Haddon-Rigg, and himself and six hundred men made prisoners, and in October of the same year the Duke of Norfolk with twenty or thirty thousand men burnt Roxburgh and Kelso and several villages, but was then compelled to retire.

It would be almost impossible now to recount the frequent greater inroads, to say nothing of the lesser or what may be called the private ones, but the Official Reports of two inroads in the years 1544 and 1545, which have been preserved, deserve some notice. No less than eleven Dickson fortalices were demolished at this time.

The first report is that of Lord Eure, Sir Brian Laiton, Sir Robert Bowes and others, entitled "Exployts don upon the Scotts from the beginning of July Anno 36 R. R. Henricé 8ᵗʰ" and the king is informed that up to the 17th Nov. 1544, they had destroyed 192 towns, towers, stedes, barnekyns, parish churches, and bastell-houses, slew 403 Scotts and took 816 prisoners, 10,383 nolt (*black cattle*), 12,492 shepe, 1,296 naggs and geldings, 200 gayt, 850 bolls of corn, and "Insight Geare."

This last item of household goods is not carried out but in one place it says "a great quantity."

Unfortunately there had been at this time an Anglo-Scottish party, which had supported the interests

of the English Monarch, but all parties finally united
in support of the independence of the realm. The
day of vengeance came, and the following spring the
Scots, although far less in number, utterly defeated
the English at Ancrum, slew eight hundred men, including their leaders Eure and Laiton, who for the
preceding nine months had signalized themselves
by their unexampled and cruel ravages, and took
one thousand prisoners.

The Earl of Hertford made an invasion with an
army of 14,000 men. His report is headed "The
Names of the Fortresses, Abbeys, Market Towns,
Villages, Towns and Places, burnt, raced and cast
down by the commandment of Therll of Hertforde
*   *   *   between the 8th and 23rd September 1545."
"Sum Total 287."

In this sum total are included seven monasteries
and frear-houses and three hospitals, among which
were the abbeys of Kelso, Melrose, Dryburgh, Roxburgh and Coldingham, and yet it is generally said
that these were destroyed by the Scottish Reformers !

The Earl's list also contains Kenetsyde, Hassyng-
tonmaynes, Mersington, Stanefawde, Headrigge,
Newtoun, Letam, Ormeston, Newbigging, Belclester
and Boughtrige, all of which were then, or at one
time at least, Dickson baronies, and must have been
places of more or less importance or they would not
have been mentioned in the Earl's report.

His roll is a sad one, _e. g._, "In Lasseden burnt 16
strong bastell Houses and sundry that held the same

slain * * * won divers strong Castell Houses
and slew all the Scottish men in the same * * *
slew 80 men, the most part being Gentlemen and of
hed surnames."

In one of the Earl's letters dated Sep. 13, 1545, he
says "not so much harm done these hundred years,"
and speaking of burning the standing corn he adds
they had employed Irishmen for the Borderers would
not burn their neighbour's property. The orders of
King Henry VIII, were in case of resistence to slay
man, woman and child, and to destroy every thing.
Sir Robert Bowes almost repeats the Earl's words,
for desirous to do his duty in what he considered a
perfect manner he drafted a hundred Irishmen into
the expedition "because the Borderers will not wil-
lingly burn their neighbours"—a very significant
remark—the English Borderers were not sufficiently
relentless to be relied on for wanton mischief and
cruelty, even although it was to serve the king.

Our clans it will be seen had sufficient provocation
and should not be censured too harshly, for they
were not a bloodthirsty race like some of the ruffians
in the Far West in this century of education, as the
contemporary evidence of a Scotch bishop (not a
Borderer), a Frenchman and an Englishman shows
that they were an honorable and kind-hearted people,
loth to shed blood—in fact, a jolly, thoughtless set
of marauders.

Bishop Leslie tells us what were their ideas of
meum et tuum, and if we have socialists in these

enlightened days, it is not surprising that communistic opinions flourished when there was almost no enlightenment at all. They considered it perfectly legitimate, aye even gallant and honorable to plun-der their English neighbours south of the border, but always, if possible, without the effusion of blood. Their chief property was in cattle, and as they were nightly exposed to the attacks of the English March-men —

> "Northumbrian prickers*, rude and wild."

As rapacious and active as themselves, their incur-sions assumed the appearance of fair reprisals. A predatory expedition was the general declaration of enmity; and the command given by the chief to clear the pastures of the enemy constituted the usual let-ters of marque, and the cattle taken were considered fair spoils of war.

When Wat of Harden in 1576, married Mary Scott of Dryhope, her father agreed to find him in victuals for man and horse at Dryhope Tower, a twelvemonth and a day, *in return for the profits of the first Michaelmas moon*, meaning the plunder of a raid into England — and this contract was drawn up by a no-tary public before witnesses! But in fact disorder of all kinds prevailed in every kingdom of Europe to a degree almost incredible. How frequently we read in old Froissart or Monstrelet of noble knights going forth in search of adventures, which in our

---

*The ancient spurs had a single spike only, and were called pryck spurs.

present language would signify to lay their hands on whatever they came across.

The robber knights of Germany were notorious. Rauber or robber (*Freiherr Rauber von Plankenstein*) is a noble German name, and de Roovere (the Robber*) a noble Dutch one, the first of whom on record was Edmond de Rovere, Lord of Rode in 1179. Ladron (Robber) de Guevara is a noble Spanish name, and in France a Captain Taillebot was ennobled in 1562, his name being probably the Romance "talebot," *i. e.*, pillager, thief. The first on record (in Domesday Book) of the English Talbots was a Talebot. . .

One must suppose that the founders of these families were leaders especially famous, like to our Johnny Armstrong, Rob Roy MacGregor or that chief of Clan Grant called James of the Forays.

A Cameron of Lochiel bore a similar *sobriquet*, Ailean nan Creach, Allan of the Forays. In his old age however in expiation of seven great forays, he built as many churches, and is therefore sometimes spoken of in tradition as Ailean nan Eaglais, Allan of the Churches.

They were not very sensitive regarding nomenclature, and some of their appellations were not dissimilar to those of the North American Indians. A Sitting Bull is living still, but how many are aware that Rollo, Duke of Normandy, was really a Walking Wolf?—Jarl Heirulff or Gangerolf, for the Earl

---

* The prefix "de" in Dutch means *the*, as de Witt, the White.

Lord Wolf was obliged on account of his great size to gang on foot as no horse could carry him. One of the Conqueror's companions was Lord with the Teeth (*Dan as denz* — what tusks he must have had), another William with the Whiskers (*als gernons*, and Algernon is still almost a hereditary baptismal name in the Percy family), a Duke of Guienne, Towhead, another noble Ass's head. A son of the Duke of Gascony, Arnoud the Unborn! One of the late Prince Albert's ancestors was Frederick with the Bitten Cheek, but a very nasty name was that of a Welsh noble, Howel the Scabby! And they were not ashamed of it for even his ~~great~~ grandson subscribed his name as Llewellyn ab Gwilym ab Hywel y grach.

But I am digressing and will only add a few Scotch *sobriquets* derived from deformities. A Marquess of Athol was known as John with the Large Mouth (Ian a Bheal mor); a Duke of the same house who was blind of an eye, Ian Cam; the second Earl of Breadalbane was John the Lame (Ian Bachach); a Macleod of Macleod Alexander the Humpback (Alasdair Crotach), and Lachlan Maclean, laird of Dowart was styled the Big-bellied (Bronach). Hugh Fraser, Lord Lovat (*b.* 1666) who had a large black spot on his upper lip, was called Black Spotted Simon's son (Mac Shimi Baldu).

But why should I go on when we find at the present day such names as Parnell, Trollope, Trull, Fitz Parnell, Cumbechance, and the like?

3

In 1377, the King of Cyprus, who paid a visit to England, was robbed and stripped there on the highway with all his retinue, and even in the very heart of good old England there was one county so noted for its robbers, who harboured in its woods until they were cut down by Leofstane, Abbott of St. Albans, .that the proverb ran

> " Buckinghamshire bread and beef,
> If you beat a bush you'll start a thief."

With these it was all on one side, but with the Marchmen of both countries there was a *quid pro quo*. They were usually called *thieves*, an expression I have not used as the word has now a different signification. A thief may be defined as one who will take whatever he can pick up and has himself nothing to lose, while their forays were commonly only a retaliation for recent injuries, or in revenge of former wrongs, and when they carried off cattle or other spoils it was with the consciousness that their own herds were exposed to the risk of being appropriated by others.

When King James charged Johnnie Armstrong with treason and robbery the border chief replied:

> " Ye lied, ye lied, now King, he says,
> Although a King and prince ye be!
> For I've loved naething in my life,
> I weel dare say but honesty.
> Save a fat horse and a fair woman,
> Twa bonnie dogs to kill a deir;
> But England sould have found me meal and mault,
> Gif I had lived this hundred yeir."

As old Satchells says (drawing a very nice distinction), they were not thieves, but freebooters.

I have never met with an account of a private Border foray, but one of a Highland raid has been preserved, which will give some idea of the lordly scale in which they were sometimes conducted, as well as the proportion of the different kinds of stock, then kept.

A Decree of Council of James V (1488–1513) is as follows:

"That Huchone Ross of Kilrawok and his son shall restore, consent and pay to Mr. Alexander Urquhart, sheriff of Cromarty, the following items, carried off by them and their accomplices:

	s.	d.
600 Cows, price of each	13.	4.
5 Score horses, each	26.	8.
50 Score sheep, each	2.	–.
20 Score goats, each	2.	–.
200 Swine, each	3.	–.
20 Score bolls of victuals, each boll	6.	8.

Six hundred cows, 100 horses, 1,000 sheep, 400 goats, etc., was the work not of thieves, but of foragers on a grand scale — *i. e.*, judging them always by the standard of the times they lived in, when religion consisted in saying a few paters and aves, every thing else being left to the priest, and Usher's eleven commandments were practically unknown.*

---

*The Archbishop had often heard of the saintly Rutherford, and when traveling in Scotland contrived to arrive at the manse at

"Reparavit cornua Phœbe" (We'll have moonlight again) was the motto of the Scotts of Harden, and "Best riding by moonlight" that of the Buccleughs. "Ye shall want ere I want" that of the Cranstouns, and "Forward" that of the Douglasses. One of the Dickson mottoes was "Fortes fortuna juvat" (Fortune favors the bold) and another "Cubo sed curo" (I sleep but watch). The Haliburton motto was "Watch well."

War-cries called Slughorns, Slogans or Ensenzies, were confined generally to chiefs of clans and military leaders. Most of them are lost, but the earliest on record, save perhaps that of Gaul Mac Morn "First to come and last to go" is that of the Celtic portion of the Scotch army at the battle of the Standard in Yorkshire, A. D. 1138, who cried "Albanich, Albanich!"* St. Andrew was the shout of the kings of Scotland; that of the old Earls of Douglas "A Douglas! A Douglas!" and of the Homes "A Home! A Home!" The Scotts cried "Bellendaine" from

nightfall, and as was formerly customary when there were few travelers, asked for accommodation. At family prayers Rutherford catechized them, and his question to the stranger was "How many commandments are there?" "Eleven" was the reply. Gravely expressing his surprise, the minister finally said, "What then is the eleventh commandment?" "A new commandment give I unto you, that ye love one another," was the answer. Rutherford soon found out who his guest was, and the following day being Sunday, requested him to take his place in the kirk, which the prelate did, using the Presbyterian form only.

*People of Albainn, or Scotchmen.

Bellendean in Roxburghshire or according to Logan "Ale Muir." The Cranstouns "Henwoodie" from their place of rendezvous on Oxnam water, and the Maxwells "Wardlaw! Wardlaw! I bid you bide Wardlaw!" from a hill near their castle of Caerlave· rock. The Setons (not a Border family, however), cried "A Seton! A Seton! Set on! Set on!"

There are two little burns called the Tarset and the Tarret and the slogan of the people of that district was "Tarsetburn and Tarretburn! Yet! Yet! Yet!"

A most singular cry of some of our Marchmen was "A holy day! A holy day!" every day in their estimation being holy that was spent in ravaging England. This is said to have been the origin of the name of the Hallidays of Allandale.

Many of the border families, English as well as Scotch, bore mullets in their arms. These in heraldry are said to be spur-rowels, and it has therefore been considered that they were emblematical, but the heralds appear to have been at fault in styling them rowels, for the Douglasses and Dicksons probably bore mullets, which are only five-pointed stars, before rowels were invented, which was only in the beginning of the fourteenth century. A mullet is represented on the seal of Adam Home, A. D. 1165. The earliest known seal of the Douglasses is of the year 1296, and bears three mullets, and these may have been assumed, for arms were seldom granted in those days, about the middle of the thirteenth century by Dick de Keth or Keith, whose mother appears to have

been a Douglas, and who was father of Thomas Dicson, born in 1247.

"Spare nought" was the motto of the Hays, ancestors of the Marquesses of Tweeddale, and if it was
adopted in 1522, when the English burned Kelso and
eighty villages besides, or in 1545, when Lord Eure
burned the tower of Broomhouse, with its lady, a
noble and aged woman, her children and whole
family,— it must be allowed the Hays had some ex-
cuse.   At the battle of Ancrum Moor the cry of our
Borderers was "Revenge for Broomhouse."

The ladies of the day were notable housewives.
When the Harden larder was empty a dish was
placed by her ladyship's orders before the baron of
Harden himself, which being uncovered disclosed a
pair of spurs—and the equivalent to the modern
order "Boot and saddle" was soon given.

This custom was peculiar to the Scotts of Harden,
but is constantly brought up against all our fore-
bears, yet no one ever adds that it was the custom in
Cumberland to lay a sword on the table when the
provisions were finished!

After 1542, the laird of Harden of that period
might have said that in that year King Henry, before
any declaration of war, seized twenty-eight Scotch
ships laden with costly merchandize, and if an English king could do that in time of peace might not a
Scotch baron pick up a few cattle?

Every evening the sheep were generally taken
from the hills and the cattle from the pastures to be

secured in the lower floors or barnekyns of the strong houses, so that the disappointed rovers often found every thing secure.

Even " the sturdy Armstrongs who were forever riding" were sometimes thus disgusted. The old lines say —

> " Then Johnie Armstrong to Willie 'gan say
> Billie, a riding then will we:
> England and us have been long at feud
> Aiblins we'll light upon some bootie.
> Then they're come unto Hutton Ha',
> They rade that proper place about,
> But the Laird he was the wiser man,
> He had left na geir without
> Except sax sheep upon a lea;
> Quo' Johnie — I'd rather in England dee
> Ere this sax sheep gae to Liddesdale wi' me."

Poor Johnie was only carrying on a private war of his own. Six sheep only, however, were beneath his notice. Those were the days when to return a Roland for an Oliver was the rule, and he said truly that with England we have been long at feud. Johnie Armstrong, Laird of Gilnockie, was famous as the most popular and potent forager of his time, who laid the whole English border under contribution, levying saufey money or blackmail as far as Newcastle, but who never injured any of his own countrymen. It was said that no one, of whatever estate, between the border and Newcastle but paid him blackmail.

He was always attended by twenty-four gentlemen well mounted. When James V made a Royal Prog-

ress in 1528, Gilnockie appeared with thirty-six persons in his train, all richly apparelled and unarmed ;
but the king, finding him in his power, and being
then at peace with England, ordered him to be executed, notwithstanding all his offers. Finding his
entreaties were of no avail, he boldly said that had
he expected such a reception he would have defied
the king and all his troops, but that it was folly to
ask grace of a graceless face.

> " To seek hot water beneath cold ice,
> Surelie it is a great folie :
> I haif asked grace of a graceless face,
> But there is nane for my men and me."

He was betrayed and put to death without trial, a
proceeding which, even in that age, was considered
unjustifiable ; but the king was then only twenty-
one years old, and was probably a tool in the hands
of Armstrong's enemies.

Lindesay of Pittscottie, speaking of the execution,
says : " Quhilk monie Scottis mene heavily lamented,
for he was ane doubtit (*redoubted*) man, and als good
ane chieftain as ever was vpoun the Borderis aither
of Scotland or of England."

There is no trace whatever of his stronghold, the
last relics of the tower of Gilnockie having been re
moved to make a bridge over the Esk. The tower
of Hollows, a square peel seventy feet high, is said
to have been his ; but Hollas Tower was held by
Lord Maxwell, and there is no proof that he ever
granted it to Gilnockie.

I repeat, then, should our clans be so loaded with reproaches? They were, at least, no worse than their neighbors on the south side of the Border.

Modern writers generally forget that the doctrine of those days was

> "The good old law — the simple plan —
> That they should take who have the power,
> And they should keep who can"—

and the Pope himself tried to play that game, for in 1300 Boniface VIII claimed to be liege lord of Scotland, but without avail. Some years later (1317) he issued a bull excommunicating the Bruce and all his adherents in the most solemn manner, but the king would not receive it neither would the Scotch bishops promulgate it and the fulminations of the Vatican were totally disregarded. The following year the Pope again ordered his legates to publish the sentence of excommunication, which was accordingly done in England, Wales and Ireland and also in France and Flanders, but again the Scotch bishops took no notice of the threats of their brother bishop of Rome. The interdict was not obeyed and although the bell was ordered no longer to be rung, the book no longer to be opened nor the candles to be burnt, nevertheless the churches were not closed, the regular services continued to be performed, and every thing went on as usual.

And we succeeded as well also in our struggles with Albion. At one time when there were internal dissensions and the country was split into two parties

4

by the rival claimants Bruce and Baliol, England
"had the power" and took possession, but the tide
turned and we were again united.

To state the case as briefly as possible.

After the death of King Alexander III, in 1285,
without male issue there were two claimants, Baliol
being favored by King Edward I, of England, who
sent an army to Scotland, took Berwick, Dunbar,
Edinburgh, Stirling and other places, appointed
Warenne, Earl of Surrey, governor of Scotland, and
after leaving garrisons behind him in the captured
places returned home, when the Scots raised a strong
force under the Earl of Buchan, the English dis-
persed in the different fortresses not daring to move ;
ravaged Northumberland and Cumberland and laid
siege to Carlisle, which, however, he was unable to
reduce. Then came the war of independence under
Wallace the saviour of his country, who after numerous exploits was joined in 1297, by Sir William
Douglas and soon after by Robert Bruce. Edward
ordered Warenne to chastise and suppress them, but
he was met by Wallace at Cambuskenneth and defeated with great loss. Wallace then returned to
the besieging of castles and in a short time so changed
the fortune of war that there remained no English in
Scotland except as prisoners. He then entered England on the first of November, remained there three
months, living upon the enemy, and returned home
on the first of the following February with much
spoil.

The English parliament ordered a general muster at Newcastle which took place in January, 1298, the number that appeared being 2,000 excellent armed horse, more than 1,200 light horse, and about 100,000 foot, who were, however, dismissed, but reassembled again in June and advanced into Scotland and in a battle at Falkirk entirely defeated the Scots with great slaughter.

Soon after, as we all know, Wallace resigned his charge as guardian of Scotland, but continued in arms asserting his freedom, until he was taken prisoner and unmercifully condemned and executed as a traitor in London in 1305.

Edward, after his victory, wasted all the country beyond the Forth as far as Perth and withdrew his army and returned to London at the end of the year. After his departure the Scots again arose and expelled all Edward's governors from the different cities and castles. Two years later (1302) Edward sent a fresh body of forces, thirty thousand in number under John Lord Segrave, who plundered the country as far as Roslin, when he unwisely divided his forces into three divisions who were attacked successively by the Scots, eight thousand in number under John Cumin and Simon Fraser, and defeated with great loss. Edward immediately raised a larger army, attacked the country by sea and land and again reduced it, appointed governors and magistrates and went back to England.

Then Bruce commenced to take a prominent part,

and, after many struggles, finally seized nearly all the castles throughout the south of Scotland. Edward I died and was succeeded by his son, Edward II, who in 1309 invaded Scotland, but accomplished nothing worthy of notice.

The next year, however, Bruce twice invaded England in retaliation, and returned with immense booty, and in the two following years recovered all the fortified places which remained in the possession of the English.

Then came the *coup de grace*, when the English army of upward of twenty thousand infantry, together with ninety-three barons with horse and arms to the amount of forty thousand cavalry, including three thousand having their horses covered with plates of mail, and the Irish Prince O'Connor with twenty-six Irish Chieftains and their followers, a body of Welsh warriors under their own chief, the Earl of Hainault, at the head of the chivalry of France and Germany, and fifty-two thousand archers, in all considerably over one hundred thousand men, besides the camp followers, the largest army that had ever left England, met the Scotch army of less than forty thousand fighting men, with over fifteen thousand unarmed camp followers, at Bannockburn in 1314, and were totally defeated, with the loss of upwards of thirty thousand men. The spoils were so enormous that an English historian (the Monk of Malmesbury) says that the chariots, wagons and wheeled carriages which were loaded with baggage and military stores would, if drawn up in a single line, have extended sixty leagues. He adds, "O day of vengeance and misfortune! day of disgrace and perdition! unworthy to be included in the circle of the year, which tarnished the fame of England and enriched the Scots with the plunder of the precious stuff of our nation to the extent of two hundred thousand pounds."

Two hundred thousand pounds of money in those days amounts to about six hundred thousand pounds weight of silver, or about three millions of pounds of our present money. Almost a bagatelle now, when referring to an army; but then a cow could be bought for five shillings, and an ox for six shillings and eight pence.

Then came our turn "to keep who can," and with the sole exception of the town of Berwick, which was ceded to England by treaty in 1482, we never gave up a foot of ground; but when the Royal Families were united by marriage, then in our kindness we gave old England a King.

Not that peace followed after Bannockburn, or that was our last victory; for in 1315 Bruce made an inroad, penetrating as far as Richmond, thence to the west of Yorkshire, wasting the country for about sixty miles, and carrying home much booty. In 1318, Sir Robert Keith, Randolph and Douglas reduced Berwick, became masters of all Northumberland except Newcastle, and returned to Scotland laden with spoils. In 1319, however, the Earl of

Murray and Lord Douglas made an invasion, committing terrible ravages, but were finally defeated with a loss of three thousand men.

Early in 1322, the English Parliament granted the king for serving in the Scottish war a foot soldier out of every village and hamlet, and a greater number out of the larger towns, but before this was effected, the Scots made an inroad in June and again in July, marching as far as Preston, eighty miles within England and returned home safely. Soon after the English invaded Scotland as far as Edinburgh, but from storms at sea preventing their ships arriving and provisions failing, for the country was deserted and desolate, they returned to England after only fifteen days. The Scots then made a new irruption, and met Edward II at Byland Abbey, Yorkshire, where he had collected his army together and added fresh levies, but he was again routed by the Bruce, and made a precipitate flight, abandoning camp equipage, baggage and treasure. The Scots plundered the country as far as Beverley and returned home laden with booty, driving large herds of cattle before them and rich in multitudes of captives. Sully, Grand Butler of France and many French knights were among the prisoners, but Bruce dismissed them not only free from ransom but enriched with presents.

In 1327, Randolph and Douglas invaded England as far as Durham with twenty-four thousand horse, and although pursued by Edward III, with an army of about sixty thousand, of whom eight thousand were horse and twenty-four thousand archers, they succeeded in returning home safe with the plunder of a three weeks' raid. At one time Edward thought he had them in his power, for behind the Scots army was stretched out a large morass which was deemed impassable for cavalry, but the Scots prepared a number of hurdles made of wands or boughs tightly wattled together, and packed up in the smallest compass their most valuable booty, and at night, leaving their camp fires burning to deceive the enemy, they threw down the hurdles upon the softer places of the bog and thus passed over the water-runs in safety, taking care to remove the hurdles so as to prevent pursuit.

In March, 1333, Lord Archibald Douglas with over three thousand men ravaged the estates of Lord Dacre in Cumberland to the extent of thirty miles, and returned without an encounter. In retaliation, Sir Anthony Lucy entered Scotland, met Sir William Douglas, and after a fierce conflict gained the victory.

In July, 1333, the English and Scottish armies met at Halidon Hill, and the latter suffered a terrible defeat, caused chiefly by the showers of arrows poured into their close battalions by the English archers. The Scots had about sixty thousand men, and the two armies were about equal in number. The Scottish loss was about ten thousand, or according to Boece, fourteen thousand, while a comparatively small number of the English suffered. The English writers represent their army as being far inferior in numbers to the Scots, and that there fell on their side only one knight, one esquire and twelve or thirteen footmen! King Edward, however, in his orders to the prelates for a public thanksgiving, though he speaks of the Scottish army as being very considerable, does not mention any inferiority of numbers on his own side, and says that the battle was gained without much loss. Had the English loss been only fifteen against nearly as many thousands, would he not have used stronger language?

In 1335, Edward and Baliol again invaded Scotland into the far North, and after making a truce with King David, and appointing a Guardian of Scotland, left the country in November. The next year the Scots arose again, Edward returned, laid Aberdeen in ashes, fortified several places and left Scotland again in September. In 1337, the Earl of March defeated a great body of English at Panmure.

After continual struggles, tiresome to relate, the English in 1342, had been driven out of every part of Scotland except Berwick, and King David Bruce entered England by the eastern marches, wasted and spoiled the counties of Northumberland and Durham and returned home, but was pursued by Edward who met him at Jedburgh, but after some days spent in skirmishing, a truce was agreed to for two years.

In 1345, the Scots invaded Westmoreland and burnt Penrith, Carlisle and other towns, but a detached party being routed, they retired. The following year, David with a large army marched through Cumberland and Northumberland as far as Durham, where they were met by the English army and routed at the battle of Neville's Cross, with a loss of fifteen thousand men, King David himself being made prisoner. Scotland was again invaded as far as Perth, when a truce was made, but as the English refused to surrender their prisoner, the Scots continually laid waste the English borders until 1356, when Edward again advanced into Scotland, and Baliol made a formal surrender into his hands of his whole right to the kingdom of Scotland. The King went as far as Haddington, but being continually harrassed by small parties of Scots and provisions failing, after burning Edinburgh and Haddington he returned home. David remained a prisoner for eleven years until 1357, when Edward finding Scotland could not be captured, released him for a heavy ransom.

In 1370, the English entered Scotland burning the lands of Sir John Gordon, who in return invaded England and seized a number of cattle. When returning to Scotland he was met by Sir John Lilborne, but after a severe combat the English were defeated and Lilborne taken prisoner. In revenge Henry, Earl of Northumberland, invaded the country with seven thousand horse and encamped at Duns, but the herdsmen and people of the country made use of a sort of machine which they usually employed to frighten away the wild cattle and deer from their corn. These were a kind of rattle made of bags of

5

dried skins filled with pebbles at the end of poles which being shaken made a hideous noise. With these they ran round the camp causing a stampede, the English horses breaking their halters and bridles, so that the enemy, not being able to recover them and finding themselves on foot, quietly returned home.

Mutual inroads of no particular note continually occurred. In 1380, William, Earl Douglas, with twenty thousand men invaded England while a large fair was being held at Penrith and returned home with great booty, in revenge of which a part of fifteen thousand English under Lord Talbot soon after entered Scotland, near the Solway, but were met in a narrow defile and defeated, great numbers being slain or drowned in the Esk. In 1383 the Scots took the castle of Wark, and the year after the Duke of Lancaster invaded Scotland, going as far as Edinburgh, but was obliged by hard weather and want of provisions to return.

In 1385, Richard II, with an army of sixty thousand, entered the country by the east coast, burnt Edinburgh, Perth, Dundee and some other places and returned home, while at the same time thirty thousand Scots entered England by the western border, plundered and laid waste the country as far as Newcastle and carried home their booty in safety.

In 1386 there was a truce, but the next year the Scots made a successful inroad on the western border. In 1388 took place the famous battle of Otterburn elsewhere referred to.

In 1398 a treaty was made between the two countries for redressing all grievances and appointment of commissioners, but there were inroads again and in 1400 Henry IV entered Scotland with a numerous army but failed in his attempt against the castle of Edinburgh and returned to Newcastle in about a month. In 1402 the Earl of Douglas invaded England with ten or twelve thousand men, but they were met and routed at Homildon by the Earl of Northumberland. Many Scottish nobles and seven hundred common men fell in this fatal engagement. No person of note fell on the English side the victory being won entirely by the archers.

In 1417, the Scots entered England, but learning that the Dukes of Bedford and Exeter were marching toward them with an army of one hundred thousand men, they returned home, and the English leaders judged it better not to follow them. About this time Sir Robert Umfraville made great devastations in Scotland for two years, burning Hawick, Selkirk, Jedburgh, Dunbar and the forests in Berwick and Teviotdale.

In 1424, a treaty was made, and King James married Lady Jane Somerset, cousin to the king of England.

A few years later, as the counties of Northumberland and Cumberland had suffered so much from the incursions of the Scots, the king of England, at the request of Parliament, remitted to them all taxes and •debts due to the crown.

In 1436, the Earl of Northumberland, with four thousand men, advanced toward the Scottish marches, but was met in his own territories by Douglas, Earl of Angus, at the head of about the same number of men, and defeated, the Scots losing about two hundred, while of the English fifteen hundred fell, of whom forty were knights and four hundred were made prisoners. Again a truce was made. In 1448, the Earls of Northumberland and Salisbury destroyed the towns of Dunbar and Dumfries, and Douglas, Lord of Balveny, in revenge, burned Alnwick and spoiled and laid waste the county of Cumberland. In retaliation, the Earl of Northumberland led a considerable army over the western march, who were met near the river Sark by the Scots, when a bloody battle ensued wherein the Scots were again victorious. Three thousand English are said to have been slain or drowned in their flight in the Frith of Solway. The loss on the side of the Scots was six hundred men.

In 1459, James II raised an army to recover Roxburgh and some other places that had been long held by the English, but was killed by the bursting of a cannon. The queen continued the siege until the garrison surrendered, and then laid waste the English marches to a considerable extent. In 1464, the Earl of Warwick burned Jedburgh, Lochmaben and many other places. In 1482, the Duke of Gloucester, the Duke of Albany and the Earl of Northumberland, with twenty-two thousand five hundred men, advanced as far as Edinburgh, where the nobility had risen against the king. A treaty was carried on by the latter and a truce concluded, in which the town of Berwick was given up to England.

In 1497 Henry VII, raised a considerable force for a war with Scotland, but was detained by an insurrection in Cornwall, when the king of Scotland seized the opportunity of entering England and ravaged the country as far as Norham, when hearing of the approach of the English army he led back his own and was followed by Surrey, who took the small castle of Ayton, but a negotiation for peace put a stop to further progress.

In 1513 a party of English made an inroad and carried off considerable booty, and soon after Lord Hume, Warden of all the marches, invaded England at the head of about three thousand horsemen, but on his return was met in an ambush by Sir William Bulmer and defeated. The Scotch king eager to avenge the defeat of his warden invaded England, took Norham and other castles and collected much booty, but King James wasted his time at Ford with the beautiful Lady Heron, so that the provisions began to fail and the army was exposed to continual rains. For this reason and to carry back their spoils great numbers of the common men deserted and the army gradually melted away until there remained not over thirty thousand when the English army of about the same number appeared. King James IV who was a brave man but not a general, against the

advice of his friends, charged on foot in the thickest
of the battle, and when he perceived that the day
was lost, seeing his standard bearer, Sir Adam For-
man, fall he pressed into the middle of his enemies
by whom he was slain. The loss of the Scotch at
this battle of Flodden was ten thousand according
to an original gazette preserved in the Herald's College, London, and Polydore Virgil says the English
lost five thousand.

About two months after, in November, 1513, Lords
Dacre and D'Arcy invaded the country at the head
of three thousand horse and three hundred infantry,
burned Rowcastle* and Langton on the Teviot,
and collected considerable booty, but on the appearance of Lord Hume with about two thousand followers the English retired.

Short truces, sometimes of two or three years were
constantly made and almost as frequently broken.

I have previously mentioned the principal inroads
made by the English in this century and will only
add that in November, 1542, a Scottish army entered
England, but they had hardly crossed the border at
Solway Moss when an order was read from the king
appointing his favorite, Oliver Sinclair, generalissimo.
This was received with the most extreme disapproba-
tion, many of the nobles declaring that they would
immediately return home, and the whole army, agitated with the discussion became a disorderly mob.
At this crisis two English leaders appeared and, be-

* This castle belonged at one time to the Dicksons.

coming sensible of the situation, attacked the Scottish camp. There was not the semblance of an engagement, for to fight might have been to secure a victory for the king's detested favorite. Upwards of a thousand yielded without striking a blow, and the rest, throwing away the weapons which they would not use, fled in disorder. The loss of killed, wounded and prisoners was over three thousand men, besides which many were swallowed up in the morass.

The last battle of any importance was that of Pinkie, near Edinburgh, in 1547, where the English had the advantage of the ground and the assistance of their fleet, and as they made good use of the cannon, both of the field and of the fleet, the Scots were seized with a sudden panic, and fled in disorder, losing some two thousand taken prisoners and over ten thousand slain.

In 1587, the Borderers again broke out into open hostility. Six successive forays swept with relentless havoc through the middle marches, and Sir Cuthbert Collingwood, the English warden, found himself too weak to restrain the incursions of Cessford, Fernihurst, Bothwell and Angus. In a piteous letter to the Secretary, Walsingham, he described the country as having been reduced to a desert, wasted with fire and sword and filled with lamentation and dismay ; but so inadequate was the assistance he received that Buccleugh, Cessford and Johnstone, with a force of two thousand men, attacked him in his castle of Eslington, slew seventeen of the garri-

son, took one of his sons prisoner, and but for the
fleetness of his horse would have taken the warden
himself.

In 1596, the English warden arrested Kinmont
Willie, a chief of the Armstrongs, on the evening of
a day of truce, an act both illegal and dishonorable,
and Scot of Buccleugh demanded that he should be
surrendered. The request being refused, Buccleugh,
with a chosen band of mounted followers, stormed
Carlisle Castle and took the prisoner back to Scotland. As he returned home, carrying the prisoner
weighed down by his chains, which they had not had
time to remove, and with all Carlisle at his heels, he
came to the swollen river.

> " Buccleugh has turn'd to Eden water,
> Even where it flowed frae bank to brim,
> And he has plunged in wi' a' his band
> And safely swam them through the stream.
>
> He turn'd him on the other side
> And at Lord Scroope his glove flung he —
> ' If ye like na my visit in merry England,
> In fair Scotland come visit me.'
>
> All sore astonished stood Lord Scroope,
> He stood as still as rock of stane;
> He scarcely dared to trew his eyes,
> When thro' the water they had gane.
>
> ' He is either himsell a devil frae hell,
> Or else his mother a witch maun be;
> I wadna have ridden that wan water
> For a' the gowd in Christentie.' "

Queen Elizabeth demanded his surrender, and the
king was finally induced to give him up.

When he appeared before the Queen, who loved bold actions, even in her enemies, she demanded of him fiercely how he had dared to storm her castle, to which the border baron, nothing daunted, replied — " What, Madam, is there that a brave man may not dare ? " Turning to her courtiers, the Queen, pleased with his reply, exclaimed : " With ten thousand such men our brother of Scotland might shake the firmest throne in Europe."

The Elliot ballad, sometimes called their Gathering, referring to Queen Mary of Scotland, must not be forgotten —

> " I have vanquished the Queen's lieutenant,
>   And made his fierce troopers to flee —
> My name is little Jock Ellot
>   An' wha daur meddle wi' me ?
>
> I ride on my fleetfooted grey,
>   My sword hanging down by my knee —
> I ne'er was afraid of a foe,
>   Then wha daur meddle wi' me ? "

Only one other verse has been preserved —

> " In raids I rode always the foremost,
>   My straik is the first in mêlée —
> My name is little Jock Ellot
>   Then wha daur meddle wi' me ? "

The brave old baron, John Elliot of Park, who had wounded the Earl of Bothwell, Queen Mary's lieutenant, evidently did not believe in the Divine Right of kings — to govern wrongly.

Leslie, bishop of Ross, before the Reformation,

6

and whose history was published in Rome in 1578, says of our marchmen —

"They think the art of plundering so very lawful that they never say over their prayers more fervently, or have more frequent recurrence to the beads of their rosaries than when they are setting out upon an expedition, as they frequently do, of fifty or sixty miles, expecting a good booty as the recompense of their devotions."

Sometimes even the clergy joined with their flocks in their plundering raids, which is not surprising when we remember that our clergy were always a very militant one. In 1306, the chaplain of King Robert Bruce, who was taken fighting at the battle of Methven was hanged, and the bishops of St. Andrews and Glasgow were sent prisoners to England in the coats of armor which they wore when taken, and at the battle of Flodden the archbishop of St. Andrews (a natural son of the king), the bishop of the Isles, the abbots of Kilwinning and Inchaffrey and others were among the slain. The statutes of James IV and V, concerning wapenschawings (weapon showings or reviews) show that the tenants of church land had no exemption, and as late as the time of Mary it was ordained that when a clergyman was slain in battle or died in the camp, his nearest relation should have the benefice.

It has been computed that before the Reformation about one-half of the wealth of Scotland was in the hands of the clergy.

The following is said to have been a prayer of the English Borderers —

> " He that ordain'd us to be born
> Send us more meat for the morn
> Part of 't right and part of 't wrang,
> God never let us fast ov'r lang,
> God be thanked and our Lady,
> All is done that we had ready."

Froissart's description of the Borderers is as follows : —

" Englishmen on the one party and Scotchmen on the other party, are good men of war; for when they meet there is a hard fight without sparring ; there is no hoo (cessation for parley) between them as long as spears, swords, axes or daggers will endure ; but they lay on each upon other, and when they be well beaten, and that the one party hath obtained the victory, then they glorify so in their deeds of arms, and are so joyful, that such as be taken they shall be ransomed ere they go out of the field ; so that at their departing courteously they will say ' God thank you.' But in fighting one with another, there is no play nor sparring."

Another old writer, quoted by Sir Walter Scott, says of the Scots, and it applied as well to the English, "that they would not betray any man that trusts in them for all the gold in England or France," and Robert Constable, an English spy, says in 1569 of his Scotch companions : "They are my guides, and outlaws who might gain their pardon by surrendering me, yet I am secure of their fidelity and have often proved it;" and Scott, in his Border Antiquities, says the marchmen were "of all others the most true of faith to whatever they had pledged their individual word. When a Borderer made a prisoner he esteemed it wholly unnecessary to lead him into actual confinement. He simply accepted his word to be a true prisoner, and named a time and place where he expected him to come and treat for his ransom."

If any one broke his word so plighted, the individual to whom faith had not been observed used to bring to the next border meeting a glove hung on the point of a spear, and proclaim to Scotch and to English the name of the offender. This was considered so great a disgrace to all connected with him that his own clan sometimes slew him.

At the bloody battle of Otterburn in 1388, the Scotch leader, the Earl of Douglas, was slain, but the English were totally defeated, and their commander, Hotspur, son of the Earl of Northumberland, and about one thousand others were taken prisoners.

Froissart says "when the Scots saw the English were discomfited and surrendering on all sides, they behaved courteously toward them, saying 'sit down and disarm yourselves for I am your master,' but never insulted them more than if they had been brothers;" and Hume of Godscroft adds: "Froysard (a stranger and favouring more the English) concluded, touching this battle, that in all history there is none so notable by the virtue of the captains and the valor of the soldiers * * *   for in the heat of the conflict no men ever fought more fiercely, in the victory obtained none ever behaved themselves more mercifully ; taking prisoners, and, having taken them, using them as their dearest friends, in all humanity, courtesy, gentleness, tenderness, curing their wounds, sending them home, some free without ransom, some on small ransom, almost all on their single word and promise to return at certain times appointed, or when they should be called upon."

The border penalties were short and sharp. Those accused of march treason were tried by jury, and, if found guilty, were decapitated; but with the marauders of either country the wardens used much less ceremony, for they were frequently hanged in great numbers, without any process of law whatever. There was an old proverb in Scotland of Jedburgh justice, where men were said to be hanged first and tried afterward. In England this was called Lydford law —

> " I oft' have heard of Lydford law —
> How in the morn they hang and draw,*
> And sit in judgment after "—

but, turning again to Leslie, speaking of the Scots, "although some things are to be noted to their dispraise, yet there are others to be greatly admired;

---

* Traitors, false coiners, etc., were often drawn or disembowelled in England.

for most of them, when determined upon seeking their supplies from the plunder of the neighboring districts, use the greatest precautions not to shed the blood of those who oppose them, for they have a persuasion that all property is common by the law of nature, and, therefore, liable to be appropriated by them in their necessity, but that murder and other injuries are prohibited by the Divine law, and if taken prisoners their eloquence is so powerful, and the sweetness of their language so winning, that they even can move both judges and accusers, however severe before, if not to mercy, at least to admiration and compassion."

Besides our ordinary jails there seem to have been a sort of honorable ones, in some places at least, for in 1597 James VI made a vigorous attempt against certain broken clans, Armstrongs, Johnstones, Bells, Batisons, Carlisles and Irvings. He came to Dum-fries, and in the course of four weeks hanged four-teen or fifteen men, and took one or two of the principal men of each branch of those clans as "pledges" that all plunder committed by their par-ticular branches should be redressed. For the re-ception of such persons in general there was a "pledge chalmer (hostage chamber)." On this occasion, however, the pledges, thirty-six in number, were distributed over His Majesty's houses, where it was ordained they should each pay 13s. 4d. weekly for their maintenance.

If the leading men generally managed to escape, although —

"Five times outlawed by
England's King and Scotland's Queen,"

the retainers, as already shown, were not always so fortunate, and usually, taking it almost as a matter of course and better than dying in their beds, when led out to execution listened calmly to the priest as he recited the so-called Neck-verse,* or Fifty-first Psalm in an unknown tongue (Latin), vainly believing that his prayers could save them.

How different would it have been could they have heard in their own dear Scotch those beautiful words which years ago I read by the request and at the bedside of a very dear friend who soon after passed away so happily, trusting not in the cross but in HIM who died upon it, and confessing to HIM alone needed no other intercessor with a God of Love.

"Have mercy upon me, O Lord, according to thy loving kindness; according to the multitude of thy tender mercies blot out all my transgressions.

Wash me thoroughly from mine iniquity and cleanse me from my sin.

For I acknowledge my transgressions and my sin is ever before me."

Although the Borderers occasionally acted as infantry they were so much accustomed to act on horseback that they considered it even mean to appear otherwise. They generally acted as light cavalry riding small sure-footed horses who could move

---

* Because said when the halter was on their necks.

through the swamps and morasses like water-fowl, and clamber like goats across a mountain pass, or up the bed of a torrent in the darkest night and through the wildest storm.   With wonderful ingenuity they had trained their horses to go upon morasses by throwing themselves on their bellies and their hoofs *roughs* and thus gaining an artificial breadth of support, to cross by short floundering leaps, ground in which ordinary horses were instantly bogged.

If the blaze of their beacon fires gave notice of the approach of an English army thousands would assemble in a single day.   The knights and esquires being mounted on able steeds, the rest on their hardy nags.   Each man carried a little bag of oatmeal trussed behind him and a griddle for baking his crakenel attacked to the crupper of his saddle, and they frequently rode in a single night or day for twenty-four miles together without bread or wine. The rivers served for drink and the cattle taken afforded meat, and instead of burdening themselves with pots they seethed their meats in the raw skins of the animals, pouring water into the bags so formed and suspending them upon stakes over the fire or roasted their beaf on spit racks before the fire.

The remark "without wine" may appear singular, but it would seem that its use was common, for Barbour, writing in 1375, that Edward the Third's army when they invaded Scotland in 1356, fell short of provisions, says "and in particular for fifteen days his army had no other drink but water," and Hall speaking of the battle of Flodden, in 1513, says of the English that they had no victuals, "and for two days before they had only drank water."

In 1490, when the Scottish admiral, Wood, attacked the English admiral, Bull, his orders were: "Charge gunners; let the cross-bows be ready; lime-pots and fire-balls to the tops; two-handed swords to the fore-rooms. * * * *Wine* was then dealt round."

Although this was not a border fight, still it should not be forgotten. Five English ships had entered the Forth and despoiled some Scottish merchantmen. Sir Andrew Wood of Largo, with his two ships, the Flower and the Yellow Carvel, attacked and took the whole five vessels. All were provided with artillery. Henry VII offered a large reward to any one who would capture Wood, and Stephen Bull with his three ships agreed to do so, and met the Scot off the coast of Fife in August. The combat continued undecided from morning until night and was renewed the following day, when at length the valor and seamanship of Wood prevailed. The three English ships were captured and taken into Dundee, where the wounded were properly attended to, and King James, besides bestowing gifts upon the English admiral and his men, sent them home with their ships as a present to King Henry!

On the approach of the enemy, the Scots were commanded by act of Parliament to "birne baillies," a term equivalent to the English bale-fires, or fires

7

to Baal, but which were afterward applied to signal or alarm fires, as " Beil fyris."

And here it may not be out of place to give some notice of the religion of our ancestors, even the pre-historic, for a history of the borders would be almost incomplete without it.

The great Pagan divinity, the sun, was worshipped all the world over with candles and torches in the temples and houses, and with fire in the open air, and was probably almost as universally known as Baal or Bel, Lord.

Tammuz, the sun-god, for whom the women wept (Ezekiel viii : 14) was the same as the Latin Bacchus, the Lamented, from the Phœnician *bakkah*, to weep. The Romans had their Baal Jupiter (Jupiter Belenus) and their Baal Apollo (Apollo Belus). The Phœni-cians worshipped him as Baal Samen, Lord of Heaven, and in Ireland he was worshipped as Beuill Samhan. The night of Halloween is called in Erse, Oidche Samhna, and in Gaelic, Samhuinn. Jerome, who lived in Palestine when the rites of Tammuz were still observed, in his *Commentary on Ezekiel,* expressly identifies him with Adonis (Adon, *Lord*), who was the same as the Northern Odin and the Mexican Wodan, where he was also known as Baal, or Bel.

His wife Astarte, the Ashtoreth of the Bible, and Ishtar of Nineveh, worshipped by the Saxons as Oster, by the Anglo Saxons as Eoster, and called by English churchmen Easter, was also worshipped as

Beltis, the Lady (*Madonna!*), and from her the Easter fires made in Scotland, even until the present century, were called Beltane, Beltis's fire, and May day is still called Beltane.

The early Christians soon commenced to amalgamate the Pagan festivals with their own, and as early as A. D. 58, Paul upbraided the Galatians for observing days and months and times and years, for they were already replacing the feasts of the demi-gods and heroes, by Saints and Martyrs. Less than two centuries after, Tertullian asked why Easter was celebrated, and Socrates, the Church Historian (fifth century), said that neither the Saviour nor His Apostles had enjoined us to keep it, but that it seemed to him *to have crept in from some old usage* — and what was that old usage except the Feast of Astarte?

The question of the time of keeping Easter long agitated the Christian Community, and it was only settled in England by a Council in 664, according to the Roman method, because as Bishop Short says "*both parties agreed that St. Peter kept the keys of heaven, and that he had used the Roman method of computing.*" (The Italics are mine.) Half a century later the Picts were also induced to adopt the Roman method.

The Pagans made their fires to Beltis on the first of May, which is probably the true date of the feast of "Our Lady" Astarte, the Syrian Venus, the Egyptian Isis. As Aphrodite her solemnities were celebrated in April. No bloody sacrifices were allowed to be offered, but only *pure fire, flowers and incense!* The festival of Flora, the goddess of flowers, was also solemnized in the same manner, from the 28th of April to the 2nd of May, and does not the Roman Church, and alas, part of the English still continue to offer these candles, flowers and incense to the Madonna — OUR LADY? Why do they not also retain the true date instead of depend-ing upon that mysterious "Full moon which happens upon or next after the 21st day of March," which may fix Easter as early as the 22nd of that month, or as late as the 25th of April?

The British Christians continued to extinguish their fires and light them again afresh with so-called "sacred" fire, obtained from the priests, long after the Pagan and Roman festivals were amalgamated.*

At the Reformation our established church of Scot-land abolished the observance of Easter day, but the church of England (who are dissenters in Scotland) not only retained it, but even made all the other feasts of their calendar depend upon it ; in relation to which it may be added that there is no authority whatever for feasts or fasts in the New Testament.

No one can tell even the season of the year, much less the day, in which our most blessed Lord was

*It must be explained here, that before the days of friction matches in the first half of the present century, so difficult was it to kindle a fire with flint and steel, that fires were never extinguished at night, but the wood embers were covered with ashes, so that the live coals could be raked out in the morning.

born, but it was not in the winter for shepherds do not remain in the fields at night then, but about the year 380, the Roman church amalgamated the nativity of our Lord with the Saturnalia or pagan festival of Saturn, the Etruscan name of the sun-god. For this the authority is undoubted. Chrysostom, in a homily delivered about the year 386, says "It is not yet ten years since the day was made known to us," and in homily No. 31, he says it was done "in order that while the pagans were occupied with their profane ceremonies, the christians might perform their holy rites undisturbed!"

Our church also abolished the observance of this festival, but the church of England still observe the day which the Romans consecrated as the birth-day of the unconquered sun — *Natalis invictis solis !*

During the carousals at the winter solstice the old Romans made one of the slaves Lord of the Household and in Scotland we had an Abbot of Unreason until the Reformation. In England, however, they did not give up their Lord of Misrule until Christmas was abolished by act of parliament in 1644.

As regards Lent it had originally nothing to do with our Lord's forty days in the desert, but was established by a pope about A. D. 130, as a fast of thirty-six days, or a tithe of the year, and was only settled at forty days by Pope Felix III, A. D. 487, but the four additional days were not generally accepted, and it was not until as late as the eleventh century that a Lent of forty days was recognized in

Scotland, and a few centuries after we got rid of it altogether.

It cannot be denied that the Reformation was more perfect in Scotland than in England, for while the English church, as well as the Lutheran, retained the celebration of Christmas, and other festivals, our church rejected them absolutely, denouncing the observance of all such days except the Lord's day as superstitious and unscriptural.

Scotland has reason to be thankful to her reformers. They probably believed that our Saviour's fast of forty days was part of his temptations and therefore no rule for us, for it was only when He was weak with hunger that the evil one made proposals to Him, and they must also have perceived that although our Saviour spoke to the Jews about their fast He never told His disciples to fast, neither did He recommend fasting. Mark does not even mention our Lord's forty days.

The compilers of the English Prayer Book could not find a single epistle for their great day, which they still called by its Romish name, Ash Wednesday, and had to fall back upon one of the lesser prophets of the Old Testament, without reminding the people that Joel foresaw an impending great drought and plague of locusts, and for that reason exhorted the Jews to fast, and this exhortation *for this particular fast only*, is still given as an authority for a stated fast of forty days in every year, even should Lent occur at a most prosperous season, and at a time, therefore,

especially adapted not for mourning but on the contrary for thanksgiving!

The redeeming point of the Prayer Book is its
thirty-nine articles and the prayers and collects, but
unfortunately while in our kirk the New Testament
is the guide, in the English kirk it is the calendar,
in which Pagan feasts and fasts, under Christian
names, abound, and the dates, with perhaps a very
few exceptions, are all fictitious; as, for instance,
St. James' day is celebrated in the Greek church on
the 30th April, and by the Armenian on the 28th
December, but in the thirteenth century it pleased
a pope to declare that it should be on the 25th
July, and accordingly the church of England still
celebrate it on that day. The Greek church observe St. Mark's day on the 11th January, and
the Coptic on the 23rd September, and as St.
Mark is said to have been martyred in Alexandria,
it would seem if either is the true date that the
Coptic is the real one. However, a pope decreed
that it should be April 25, and so it remains in the
English calendar, where, too, they boldly acknowledge the Roman Madonna and Queen of Heaven as
their LADY also! In the Lessons Proper for Holy
Days we read "Annunciation of OUR LADY!"

In Pagan Rome the 25th of March was the day
observed in honor of Cybele, the Great Mother of
the Gods, and in the seventh century its name was
changed to the Annunciation, and that day is still
observed by the English church, although no one

knows when the Angel Gabriel made the announcement.

The ancient Romans held a feast on the 1st or 2nd of February to Juno Februata, which was celebrated with candles and torches, and Moresin says that in Scotland the people used to run about the mountains with lighted torches like the Sicilian women in search of Proserpine. In 526 (some say 540) the pope ordained that they should close the festival by going to the churches and offering up their candles to the Virgin. It was, therefore, called Candle-Mass, and Juno's day is still celebrated by English churchmen as the Day of the Purification! These are but specimens.

When the Prayer Book was revised in Ireland a few years ago they swept away nearly all the feasts and fasts, but Cybele's Day (*Our Lady* of the Annunciation) and Juno's (*Our Lady* of the Purification) are Red Letter Days, or First-Class Festivals (!!) of the Protestant church of England, with special collects, epistles and prayers, and it was for that reason only they were retained by the sister church.

It is true we have our so-called patron saint, and his memory is respected as that of one of our Lord's apostles, but not revered; neither is his day religiously observed.

It is a curious fact that the so-styled St. Andrew's cross is a fable of the middle ages, for he is said to have been crucified in Greece, and in the Greek Menologies and in one or two Western Martyrologies he is depicted as executed on a cross of the ordinary form.

Rivers and fountains were dedicated to the sun-god Tammuz, which accounts for the many so-called holy wells still in existence, and the Thames, Tamar, Tame and Teme probably derived their names from him. The cross (**T**) was his initial and emblem, and the Druids made enormous crosses of oak trees, seeking one sufficiently adapted and cutting off all but the two principal branches, or otherwise they fastened a cross beam to the tree. They also built cruciform temples and cairns, and there is still standing at Callernish in the Lewis a Druidical temple three hundred and eighty feet long in the shape of what later became known as the Iona cross, but which is in reality the cross of Tammuz surrounded by his circle of the sun. The celebrated cairn at New Grange, Ireland, is also cruciform.

Although a Christian church was established in Rome before the arrival of Paul, the Pagan temples were not entirely abolished until about A. D. 500, prior to which, but long after the time of the apostles, the Pagan cross was adopted by the Roman church and called the cross of Christ to draw the heathen into the church by making them believe there was little difference between the two religions, but St. Paul many years after our Lord's death called it the emblem of the curse, and the second commandment forbids all emblems for the use of religion.

8

In Britanny a Roman Catholic Priest is still called by the old Pagan title, Belek, servant of Baal. Many local names in the British Isles commence with the name. There was probably a Druidical temple at Baltimore in Ireland, for the name is evidently Baal-ti-mor, the great house of Baal. He was also known as Gran or Grian, the Shiner or Sun. The Cam was anciently called Grant and Cambridge Grantabryg. The Irish Druids called the Zodiac Beach Grian, the Revolution of Grian and the Solstices Grian stad or Grian's stopping places. The Grampians, anciently Granze bene, are Grian's hills, and if further proof is necessary history tells us the Romans adopted the God's of other nations, although it seems more probable that they acknowledged them as their own under other names, and a Roman altar was discovered at Musselburgh in the Lowlands in 1565, dedicated to Apollo Granno, and Apollo was another form of the Sun God.

But the Pagans knew not who they worshipped. Bacchus had so many appellations that according to Sophocles he was called the many named, and Isis was called Myrionyma, the goddess with ten thousand names. Their wise men believed that all the gods were originally the same. It is expressly so declared it the Orphic Hymns. In them they sang to the Universal Zeus. "Zeus is the male, Zeus is the immortal female," and Arnobius tells us they sometimes prayed "Oh Baal, whether thou be a god or goddess hear us."

They desired to find the only God, but their religion had become so fearfully corrupted that they knew not where to seek Him, and as we all know the learned Athenians, and probably other nations also, built an altar

To the Unknown God!

The place from which the Highland Clan Grant derive their name is called Griantach, or Sliabh Grianus, the heath of Grian. His day was SUN-day, and even within the memory of man libations of milk were placed on Sundays in hollow stones called granni stones, of which there was one in every village. The reason of course forgotten, but the ceremony maintained even as too many still honor the Syrian Venus, who it was believed was hatched out of an egg. She was worshipped at Cyprus under the form of a large oval stone. Pliny describes what were considered the virtues of Astarte's egg, and says the Druids wore them made of chrystal and set in gold around their necks as badges of their office. He says they were made by snakes, and called snake or serpent stones (*ovum anguinum*). They are still sometimes found in Wales, made generally of some glass or vitreous paste, and are also called there to this day snake stones (*Gleini nadroedd*). Two of rock chrystal are still in existence in Scotland, one being in the royal scepter and the other is in the possession of a Perthshire family. Hindus, Chinese and Japanese have their mystic eggs, and who that has visited the Levant has not noticed the ostrich eggs suspended in the mosques ? What then is the Easter egg but a memento of that impure goddess Venus, who was the same as the great Diana of the Ephesians.

Crosses made of rowan, or mountain ash, are still sometimes placed upon cow-byres in the Highlands, being now considered a protection against witches. The rowan was, however, a sacred tree of the Druids, and is the same as the Scandinavian yggdrasil, the great ash or mundane tree, the chief and holiest seat of the gods, where they assembled every day in council. It is the same as the irminsul, the sacred tree of the Germans, from which Pagan origin is derived their Christbaum and the English Maypole.

Fires were carried round the fields in the Highlands to ensure good crops, and *Tein egin*, or Need Fires, were made when the cattle were diseased. These need fires were made in a peculiar manner, differing, however, slightly in some districts.

Without doubt all these practices formerly existed in the Lowlands, but they lingered longer in the remote Highlands.

There are prehistoric relics in Scotland which have not been preserved elsewhere, and which I ventured to point out as pre-christian some years ago, although such origin was not then, I think, ever hinted at by others.

I refer to the standing crosses at Meigle, Glammis and elsewhere, bearing sculptured figures of serpents (and Tammuz, or Grian was the serpent sun-god, a

corrupted tradition of the serpent of Paradise), a
boar (sacred to the sun-god, whose day was the winter solstice, and although the animal is no longer
sacrificed, boars' heads are still served up at Windsor
and Oxford on Christmas) ; a sow (sacred to Frigga
in Scandinavia and to Ceres in Rome) ; a long-legged
hound (and Ceridwin, the great goddess of South
Britain, was fabled to have transformed herself into
a greyhound); a centaur with a battle axe in each
hand instead of a bow; Venus' looking glass or
mirror with lily handle (the lily of Isis and Juno, and
now the Roman Catholic emblem of the Virgin),
and also with a cross handle like the sign of the
planet, elephants, *fishes*, etc.

Bacchus was sometimes called the Fish (*Bacchus
Ichthus*) and Jerome calls him the Lamented Fish
(*Piscem Mœroris*). The Philistines worshipped him
as the Fish On (*Dag On*). Joseph's father-in-law
was Priest of On (the Sun), whose city is to this day
called, by the Greek translation of its Egyptian
name Heliopolis, the City of the Sun.

One Scottish stone bears a man and a woman with
a tree between them which might be taken for Adam
and Eve, but there is a similar design at Philœ, and
these two probably represent the Celtic and the
Egyptian versions of the Latin Hercules in the garden of the Hesperides.

Compare also the man tearing open the jaws of the
lion in Wilson's Prehistoric Scotland with the Assyrian
Hercules wrestling with a lion in Layard's Nineveh.

Where did our prehistoric fellow-countryman obtain his models? There were no lions in the Land o'Cakes when that stone was carved. His forefathers brought their traditions from Babylon "which hath made all the earth drunken," and they must have brought their drawings too! But how, was it on their bodies only? We know that the Caledonians had their bodies covered with the figures of animals *α* colored blue with wo∅d, so that the Romans called them *picti* or painted men, and have we not relics of that custom also. The Picts painted their whole bodies with representations of different animals, a custom that must have originated in a warmer clime than Caledonia. Our sailors now however only tattoo their arms and sometimes their breasts.

Besides the stationary beacon fires the Borderers also formerly sent around a signal called the Fyrecross, somewhat similar to and undoubtedly a corrupted form of the Highland fiery-cross. This fyre-cross was a wisp of straw or tow, or a turf, burning or burnt, mounted on the top of a spear and carried through the country with the utmost celerity, and all men between eighteen and fifty-six, or according to some writers between sixteen and sixty, were obliged to hasten to the place of danger.

In the Highlands it was called crois-tara, crois-tarich or cran-tara, and has been supposed to signify the cross of shame (*tara*), in allusion to those who should neglect to join the banner of their chief. Jameson however, who defines it as a "stake of wood one end dipped in blood and the other burnt, as an emblem of fire and sword," says the final word is perhaps *tara*, a multitude. It was however originally a cross formed of two pieces of wood tied together, the extremities of which were *seared in fire and extinguished in the blood of a goat which was killed by the chief himself with his own sword.* Sometimes one of the ends of the horizontal piece only was burnt and a piece of linen or white cloth stained with blood was suspended from the other; and some years ago I expressed the opinion that the original signification had been long forgotten and that the crois-tara was the cross of Taran or Thoran, the God of Thunder, who was identical with the Scandinavia Thor who was considered the helper of both gods and men, and whose weapon was a fylfot cross. Moreover the goat was sacred both to Bacchus and to Mars, the God of War, and undoubtedly likewise to Thor, the God of War as well as of Thunder, as his car was drawn by two goats, and therefore in Scotland to Taran, and the case then is perfectly clear. No Highland Chieftain would turn his Andrea Ferrara into a butcher's knife, but in this event it became a sacrificial knife and he a successor of the Pagan priest offering up a sacrifice to Taran. This accounts for the blood, and the rest is equally clear for the *cross of Thor was a fiery cross* which he himself could only hold with a steel glove. Taran's cross must have been the same.

In the Orkneys the fiery cross was called the Cors or Corse, *i. e.*, Cross, and in later times it was sometimes used for calling the people to church or for other lawful purposes.

The ancient Goths, the Swedes and probably other nations had a similar custom and from the imperfect accounts that have been handed down they appear to have used rods burnt at one end, with a rope or piece of white cloth stained with blood at the other. As the cross was delivered from hand to hand, and each bearer ran at full speed, proclaiming aloud the place of meeting, a clan was assembled with great celerity. The last time it was used in Scotland was during the Rising of 1745, when it was carried about in the Highlands, and it went round Loch Tay, a distance of thirty-two miles, in three hours.

I must again confess that there was a class infesting the borders who must not be confounded with some of the Border Clans, and in favor of many of whom little can I fear be adduced.

The land lying along the Borders was called the Debateable land or Threepland, from "threep," to contend or quarrel. As early as 1222 a commission was appointed to mark out the line of frontier, and in 1450, it was agreed to render part of it a common pasture where each nation might have liberty to graze cattle, and was occupied from sun rising to sun setting, on the understanding that any thing left there over night should be fair booty to the finder.

It extended the whole length of the borders, and in proportion as the land was waste or barren its breadth was the wider, but in 1552, it was decided to divide the *Terra contentiosa* by a boundary line ; the ground on one side to belong to England and that on the other to Scotland.

Not only hordes of broken clans and broken men, but also murderers and the like resided there, many of whom harrassed both countries.

> "And stole the beeves that made their broth
> From England and from Scotland both."

Such was their dexterity that they could twist a cow's horn or mark a horse so that its owner could not know either again, and one of their pretty games was with the consent of a neighbor to carry off and sell his horse at a good distance, and after pocketing the money to steal back the horse and return him to his owner.

The Tarras Moss was one of their places of refuge. In 1598 Sir Robert Carey, the English Warden built a fort on Careby Hill to watch some of the Baitablers who had fled there, but while he was lying in wait they sent a party into England and harried his lands, and on their return sent him one of his own cows, telling him that fearing he was short of provisions they had sent him some English beef.

They were often proclaimed. A decree of the year 1567 reads as follows :

9

" Forasmikill* as it is understand to my Lord Regent and Lordis of Secrete Counsall how the thevis and brokin men inhabitantis of the contreis of Liddisdaill, Ewisdaill, Eskdaill and utheris boundis on the Marches of this realme foranent Ingland, hes nocht onelie committit divers thiftis, reiffis,† heirschippis‡ and slauchteris upoun the peciabill and gude subjectis of the Incuntre bot als hes takin sindry of thame and denenit§ thame as lauchfull presonaris or ransont or latten them to souertie agane   *   *   *   And   *   *   *   quhen‖ ony cumpanyis of thevis or brokin men cummis over the swyris¶ within the Incuntre, that all our Soverane Lordis liegis dwelland in the boundis quhairthrow thai resort incontinent cry on hie, raise the fray and follow thame alsweill in their inpassing as outpassing on fute and horsis and follow thame and the gudis reft and stollen be thame for the recovering and redding thairof * * * "

Bloodhounds were generally used in the pursuit of these marauders. When the injured parties raised the hue and cry and followed with horse and hound, it was called the hot trod or tred, and in chasing the thieves they were allowed to cross the frontiers of both countries.

---

* Forasmuch.

† Robberies.

‡ Ruin, wrecking of property.

§ Detained.

‖ When. Qu is equivalent to w.

¶ Hills or passes between the mountains.

Besides the royal and other castles on the Borders, there were also bastel-houses, or bastilles, and towers called peels, inhabited by the lairds and gentry, whether heads of clans or distinct families. Some were surrounded by barnikins or inclosures of stone, the walls whereof were, according to statute of A. D. 1535, a yard thick and six yards in height, surrounding a space of at least sixty feet. This was the minimum, but they were often stronger. These barnikins were for men of one hundred pounds a year or more, a not inconsiderable sum then, for forty years later the English master of the ordnance of the northern parts received at 5s. per day only £91, 5s. per annum, and the salary of Lord Hundsdon, warden of the east marches, was only four hundred pounds.

Men of smaller rent were to build peels and "great strengths," or strong houses.

The entrance to the tower was usually secured by two doors, the outer one of grated iron and the inner one of oak clenched with nails. The apartments were placed directly over each other, accessible by a turnpike stair easily blocked up and defended. The dependents generally lived in adjacent cottages, or huts with walls of stone, turf or mud, and when the alarm was sounded they unthatched and dismantled their cabins, so that there was nothing to burn, and huddled the women and children, the horses, cattle and sheep within the castle walls, and either joined them there, if the fortalice itself was attacked, or rode off to join in the fray.

Upon a sudden attack from any small party these bastilles afforded good means of defense, but when, as often happened, the English entered the frontier with a regular army supplied with artillery, the lairds usually took to the woods or mountains, with their most active and mounted followers, and left their habitations to the fate of war, which could seldom do any permanent damage to buildings of such rude and massive construction as could neither be effectually ruined by fire or thrown down by force, until at least when gunpowder began to be used for the purpose.

Few of these fortresses now remain. They were inconvenient for modern residences, and have been mostly cleared away. The largest peel on the Border still in existence is that of Borthwick, built in 1430, the tower of which is one hundred and ten feet high and the walls twelve to fourteen feet thick. It had six stories.

Rude as they appear to have been, a list of the furniture of one of them in the sixteenth century shows a certain degree of refinement. It consists of the "spuilzie" (spoils) of the house of Robert Ker of Ancrum, County Roxburgh, ancestor of the Marquess of Lothain, in 1573, with the valuation of each separate article, he having appealed to the king and council against certain parties for damages.

Among other articles enumerated are four silver tassis (*cups*), each weighing twelve ounces, one silver macer* double over gilt, weighing eighteen ounces, two dozen silver spoons weighing one and a half ounces each, two silver salt vats, one partially gilt with cover, weighing twelve ounces, the other weighing seven ounces. A silver foot to a cup weighing five ounces. Three dozen Flanders pulder plaittis † (*pewter plates*), five dozen Flanders poyder truncheons (*trenchers*), besides basins, washbasins, tin flagons of Flanders work, three stands napery ‡ (*table linen*) of fine dernick (*Doornick or Tournay*) work, three stands of small linen cloth, "XL furneist fedder beddis with scheittis, coveringis, coddis (*pillows*), bousteris, blankattis," three gentlewomen's gowns, to-wit, one of black champlot silk, another of French black and the third of Scotch russet, all trimmed with velvet, three gentlewomen's hats, one of black velvet, another of black armosy taffatie and the third of black felt, three men's doublets, one of black satin, another of violet armosie taffatie and the third black bombassy, etc., etc., together with one tun of wine, to-wit, three puncheons of claret, and one puncheon of white wine, "price of the tun lxvi li xiii s. iiii d,"§

---

* Macers were generally made of maple wood, one serving the entire company, as the Loving cup is still passed round in England.

† Tin or pewter plates took the place of wooden ones in the reign of James the First (1424–1437), about which time a noted tavern in Paris bore the sign of the Tin plate.

‡ James I in his Poem "Peblis to the Play," mentions a tavern in Peebles with fair table linen and a regular score on the wall. The reckoning two pence halfpenny apiece.

§ £66 13s. 4d. These were Scotch pounds then less in value than English.

and also salt meat, cheese, butter, meal, barley, oats, etc.

Such is the claim, but it can hardly escape notice that while there were forty beds completely furnished and equal to about sixteen hundred bottles of wine, there were parts only of three men's and three women's dresses, so that it would seem as if some articles had either been taken away by the owners or had not been discovered by the raiders.

This was the house of a baron only, but the inventory a century earlier of the royal plate and jewels of King James the Third, who died in 1488, impresses one with no contemptible idea of the riches and splendor of the court.   Together with a large sum in gold angels, ryders (of the Low Countries), rials (of France), unicorns and rose nobles occur "a book of gold like a table and on the clasp of it four pearls and a fair ruby ; the great diamond with the diamonds set about it ; several great and small gold chains; a collar of chalcedon, collars and beads of gold, strings of pearls, a purse made of pearls, crosses set with precious stones, numerous rings in rolls — *e. g.*, "Item a roll with seven small ringis diamantis rubeis and perle."   "Item ane uther roll with ringis in it of thame (among them) thre gret emmorantis a ruby a diamant, and other rolls of rings set with saffer, ammorant, topas, turcas and berial, together with plates, dishes and basins silver over gilt," etc., etc., and in the inventory of James V, who died in 1542, occurs *inter alia* a basin of gold weighing ten pounds.

An inventory of such things as were left in the Castle of Caerlaverock, Co. Dumfries, in 1640, affords a good idea of the wealth and luxury that characterized some of the noble mansions of Scotland at that period.

Four barrels of "seake" (Falstaff's favorite wine) and three hogsheads of French wine only remained in the wine cellar, but among numerous other articles were five suits of hangings, each estimate at three score pounds sterling. Five beds, two of silk and three of cloth, every bed consisting of five coverings * * * with silk fringes, broad silk lace, chairs and stools answerable laid with lace and fringe, with feather bed and bolster, blankets and rugs, pillows and bedstead of timber answerable; every bed estimate to be worth one hundred and ten pounds sterling.

Ten lesser beds, four with cloth curtains and six with stuff or serge, every bed furnished with bottoms, valence and testers, feather bed, bolster, rug, blankets and pillows and bedstead of timber; every bed estimate to fifteen pounds sterling.

Seventy other beds for servants, consisting of feather bed, bolster, rug, blankets, and estimate to seven pounds sterling apiece.

Forty carpets, estimate "overheid" to forty shillings sterling apiece.

Furniture of a drawing-room of cloth of silver, consisting of an entire bed * * * wardrobe and six stools, all with silk and silver fringe, estimate to one hundred pounds sterling.

Two dozen chairs and stools covered with red velvet, with fringes of crimson silk and gilt nails, estimate to three score pounds sterling.

Five dozen Turkey work chairs and stools, every chair estimate to fifteen shillings sterling, and every stool to nine shillings sterling.

A library of books " qlk stood my lord to two hundred pounds sterling" (Maxwell, Earl of Nithsdale, was a literary man and commonly called The Philosopher, which accounts for the large stock of books for that period).

Two trunks full of Holland shirts, etc., etc., damask table cloths, forty pair of sheets, seventy stands of napery, etc. Two trunks of coarse sheets and napery.

A trunk with eight suits of apparel, some of velvet, some of satin, some of cloth, etc. There was also one iron window and six cases of windows. Glass was then still so expensive that the windows were removed from unoccupied rooms.

My lord and my lady's pictures.

The bed in my lord's chamber is described as furnished of damask and laid out with gold lace. My lady's chamber is mentioned, but the furniture is not given.

Of arms there were left 22 pikes, 13 lances, 28 muskets, 28 bandoleers, 2 two-handed swords and 9 collars for daggers.

The ledger of Andrew Halyburton, a Scotch merchant residing in the Low Countries between the years 1492 and 1503, has fortunately been preserved.

Among other articles shipped by him to Scotland were " 2 poncionis (*puncheons*) off claret wyn, 2 puns (*puncheons*) Orleans wine, a stek (*piece or cask*) of Ryns wyne, 3 puns wine, a pipe of claret, a town (*tun*) of Gaschon claret, 2 bottis (*butts*) Malwissy (*Malmsey*)," etc., together with such luxuries as " 25 cassis sucur weand 28 li (*pounds*), 12 li pepar, 2 li gyingar, a li of kaneyll (*cinnamon*), 1 li clois (*cloves*), 2 li notmogis, 2 li massis (*mace*), 12 li scrozattis (*confections*), 2 barellis of applis, xii li of deytis," etc., and also the *Trois Mendiants,* viz., " fegis, raisinis and almondis."

A century later, in the Highlands, Simon Fraser, eighth Lord Lovat, imported wines, sugar and spices from France in return for the salmon produced in his rivers. He was celebrated for a liberal hospitality. The weekly expenditure of provisions in his house included seven bolls of malt, seven bolls of meal and one of flour. Each year seventy beeves were consumed, besides venison, fish, poultry, kid, lamb, veal and all sorts of feathered game in proportion. When he died in 1631, five thousand armed followers and friends attended his funeral, for all of whom there was entertainment provided.

Sir Duncan Campbell of Glenurchy, ancestor of the Marquess of Breadalbane, who died the same year, supported a similar menage. His wine, brought from Dundee, was claret and white wine, old and new, and he had three kinds of ale—ostler ale, household ale and best ale.

10

Fynes Morysin who visited Scotland in 1598, says,
"They drink pure wines, not with sugar as the
English ; yet at feasts they put comfits in the wine
after the French mánner ; but they had not our vint-
ner's fraud to mix the wines.

Another English traveler, in "A Short Account
of Scotland, London, 1702," says "their drink is
beer, sometimes so new that it is scarce cold when
brought to the table. But their gentry are better
provided, and give it age, yet think not so well of it as
to let it go alone, and therefore add brandy, cherry
brandy, or brandy and sugar, and this is the nectar
of their country, at their feasts and entertainments,
and carries with it a mark of great esteem and affection. Sometimes they have wine, a thin-bodied
claret, at ten pence the mutchkin which answers to
our quart." It is not clear what kind of "gentry"
this writer refers to for as I have shown the lords
and barons drank not only claret, but also rhenish,
malmsey and sherry wines, and bought them by the
cask, pipe or butt and hogshead or puncheon, and
not by the quart.

It is strange these authors do not mention whisky
which was known in Ireland when Henry the Second
invaded that country in 1172, when the inhabitants
were in the habit of making an alcoholic liquor
called *uisge-beatha*, synonymous with the Latin *aqua
vitæ*, water of life or *usquebaugh, i. e.*, whisky, and
Hector Boece (A. D., 1527) says of his ancestors
that when they "determined of a set purpose to be

merie, they used a kind of aquavite, void of all spice, and onelie consisting of such herbs and roots as grew in their own gardens, otherwise their common drink was ale: but in time of warre when they were inforced to lie in campe, they contented themselves with water as rediest for their turnes."

Simon Fraser, twelfth Lord Lovat, decapitated in 1747, was one of the last who kept up the old feudal state. Numbers of the vassals were about the house and entertained at the chief's expense. The principal guests sat toward the head of the table and had French cookery and drank claret; next to these were the duine-uasals* who drank whisky punch; the tenants who were beneath these were supplied with ale, and at the bottom and even outside a multitude of the clan regaled themselves with bread or an onion, or perhaps a little cheese and table beer. All clansmen are cousins and Lovat addressing one would say "Cousin ———, I told the servants to hand you wine, but they tell me ye like punch best," and to others "Gentlemen, there is what you please at your service, but I send you ale as you prefer it."

One of Lord Lovat's neighbors, Forbes of Culloden, kept a hogshead of wine constantly on tap near the hall door for the use of all comers.

The Peerage of Scotland is perhaps the most aristocratic body in the world; all creations ceased at

---

* Gentlemen, generally tacksmen or tenants (goodmen), acknowledged relations of their lord.

the period of the Legislative Union in 1707, and only two or three of the families of whom it is com posed are not of old Baronial descent, and as the title of Laird frequently occurs herein I may explain that the lesser Barons or Lairds were hardly to be distin-guished from the nobility, who, until about the mid-dle of the seventeenth century consisted of Earls and Lords only, the Ducal denomination having been mostly confined to the Royal Family.

In the Parliament of 1488, there were four Bishops, six Abbots, four Priors, eight Earls, fourteen Lords, thirty-four Barons or Lairds, and eleven Commis-saries of Burghs.

The Lairds were not only denominated from their estates, but up to a late period they used a titular signature as well as the Peers, or rather greater Bar-ons, as the former word hardly applies to Scotland where the "Peers" never had a separate house, nor had they any privileges over the lesser Barons. All were *Pares* or Peers in Courts of Justice. While there was no House of Commons there was no House of Peers. Every *tenant in capite* or landed gentle-men holding of the crown might sit and vote.

The lairds corresponded in a measure with the English lords of manors, but with greater powers; for in Scotland, as a rule, they were lords of regality, and possessed the power of pit and gallows, or juris-diction over those of their vassals or tenants who resided on their estates. Drowning was an old mode of punishment, and the right of *fossâ et furcâ* consisted in inflicting death either by drowning of women or hanging of men. Treason, it is said, did not fall under their cognizance ; but it would seem that the king himself could not arrest traitors within their territories, for as late as 1571, and again in 1574, several heads of clans, amongst whom are those of Clan Dickson, pledged themselves to keep good rule, and to apprehend not only thieves but also any traitors found within their borders.

Lord and laird are both rendered "dominus" in Latin. A tract of land with the owner's bastille, peel or mansion upon it was styled a lairdship, and the owner was not called by his name as Scot, but by his lands, as " Buccleugh."

In 1429, persons possessed of a yearly rent of twenty pounds, or of moveable goods to the value of one hundred pounds, were ordered to be well horsed and armed "from head to heel," as became their rank as gentlemen ; whilst others of inferior wealth, extending to ten pounds only in rent, or fifty pounds in goods, were bound to provide themselves with (a headpiece ?), gorget, rere and vam braces, breastplate, greaves and leg splints and gloves of plate or iron gauntlets. Every yeoman whose property amounted to twenty pounds in goods was commanded to arm himself with a good doublet of fence or a habergeon, an iron hat or knapscull, a bow and sheaf of arrows, a sword, buckler and dagger. The second rank of yeomen, who possessed only ten pounds in property, were to provide themselves with a bow and sheaf of arrows, a sword, buckler and dagger, whilst the lowest rank of all, who had no skill in archery, were to have a good "suir" hat, a doublet of fence, with sword and buckler, an axe also, or at least a staff pointed with iron.

This shows the relative value of coin when a man's wealth, as in the days of Abraham, consisted chiefly in his extensive lands and flocks. Out of an income of twenty pounds a gentleman had to be armed cap-a-pie and to own a good horse besides.

In 1540, James V ordered that every *nobleman*, such as earls, lords, knights, barons and persons exceeding one hundred pounds in yearly rent, should use white or plate armor, light or heavy as they chose, and weapons becoming their rank ; that those of a smaller income in the Lowlands have a jack of plate, halbrik or brigantine, gorget or pisan with splents, knee-pans of mail and gauntlets of plate or mail ; that unlanded gentlemen and yeoman have jacks of plate, halbriks, splents, sallat or steel bonnet with pisan or gorget, and all to wear swords. No weapons are to be admitted to wapenschawings (*weapon showings or reviews*) except spears, pikes of six ells in length, leith axes, halbards, hand-bows and arrows, cross-bows, culverins and two-handed swords. Burgesses are to arm in the same proportions of their income. Those worth one hundred pounds in goods in white armor; those under, but who may yearly spend ten pounds, like the yeomanry.

Of firearms, culverins alone are mentioned. In 1541, however, a statute was passed ordering all persons of property, not even excluding the clergy, to have hagbuts, culverins, powder, lead, etc., according to their income.

In 1590, it was decreed that no baron, in repairing to the king's presence or to justice's courts and conventions at Edinburgh, should be accompanied by more than five persons, unarmed, while lords were not allowed more than eight and earls not above twelve. The following year, however, they were permitted to have "every erll xxiiii personis or within, every lord xvi personis or within and every barroun x personis or within,—all in peceable and quiet manner, without armour and chieflie without daggis, pistolettis and utheris ingynis of fyre werk except it be shown to his Majesty that it be necessary and his Hienis special license had for their cuming when they shall be allowed to wear sword and quhinzeair (whinger or hanger)."

Vassals were only second to barons and free holders of the crown. They generally held their lands free of all service and paid only a nominal quit rent. These tenants, although holding their lands from overlords, were themselves often chiefs of clans or branches of clans, and independent of their landlords as regarded feudal superiority, and their followers acknowledged no superior save their chief. They and their ancestors had occupied their farms for generations, and the birth of the better class was as

good, and their genealogy as old, as those of the
chief himself, to whom they were mostly blood relations, and to whom they were attached with the most
unshaken loyalty. Some of them were naturally
poor, however, and they are so styled in a letter from
the English privy council to their ambassador in
France in 1547. "The Scots having of late made
many and cruel incursions, the Lord Warton, lord
warden of the West Marches, had been compelled to
make reprisals, and has taken in an ambush the Laird
Johnson, a notable Borderer of the Scottish side,
with seven or eight mean gentlemen and 120 or 140
common soldiers of his party."

Lord Wharton was not so fortunate the following
year, when he and his army of three thousand men
were defeated and the remainder retreated to Carlisle.

These poor gentry were sometimes styled bonnet-
lairds or cock-lairds. They were followed by the
husbandmen (*husbandi*), who were not serfs nor
bondsmen ; neither were they free tenants, but actual
cultivators of the land — sub-tenants.

The carls bonds, serfs or villeins were anciently in
a state of perfect servitude and were at the absolute
disposal of their landlords. They were transferred
with the lands and might be caught and be brought
back if they attempted to escape like a stray ox or
sheep. In 1170, Earl Waldev of Dunbar in a deed
of four lines made over a whole family " I give and
bequeath to the Abbot and monks of Kelso, Hadden

and his brother William and all their children and all their descendants."

Villeynage was discontinued before the beginning of the sixteenth century and before it was given up in England. This class then became cottars or sub-tenants without any tenure except that which arose out of the necessity of having men who could render services both military and agricultural.

The heritable or hereditable jurisdictions were not however abolished until 1748, and this broke the chain of feudalism which until then had curbed the progress of the people. Many claims were made for the loss of these rights or regalities, the largest being that of the Duke of Hamilton, who claimed £38,000, while the Duke of Roxburgh only demanded £4,000. The Marquess of Lothian, the Countess of Eglinton, Maclean of Cadboll, Dickson* of Kilbucho and others asked for £1,000 each; Sir John Anstruther, Car-michael of Tilleboddy, Sir Robert Dickson of Sorn-beg and others wanted £500 each, Sir James Sharp and a few more £100 each, and one only claimed less than that sum.

A few lists of Borderers and Border Clans, more or less complete have been preserved, the earliest being a record of the Barons and Clans of the West Border who submitted to the English in the dismal

---

* Dickson of Buhtrig was then extinct, and as Dickson of Bel-chester was out in the Fifteen his family were probably too well known as Jacobites for them to expect any claim of theirs, if made, would be listened to.

II

year 1547, and were for some time in subjection to
the English Government.

Of this I have seen three copies slightly differing
from each other. It is especially interesting as it
gives the numbers of the different clans, at least of
those who took the oath of fealty, which could not
always have been the entire clan as the Eliots only
number seventy-four.

ANNERDALE.

Laird of Kirkmighel...................... 222
"   Rose (*Ross**) 165
"   Hempsfield (*Charteris of Amisfield*). 163
"   Home Ends (*Carruthers of Holmains*) 162
"   Wamfrey (*Johnstone*).... 102
"   Dunwoddy (*of that Ilk†* or *Maxwell?*) 44
The Lairds of Newby and Gratney (*Johnstone*). 122
Laird of Tinnell (*Maxwell of Tinwald*)...... 102
Patrick Murray 203
Christie Urwin (*Irving*) of Coveshawe........ 102
Cuthbert Urwin of Robgill............... .. 34
Urwens of Sennersack (*Pennersacs*) 40
Wat Urwen 20
Jeffrey Urwen 93
T. Johnston of Coites 162
Johnstones of Craggyland.................. 37
Johnstones of Driesdell (*Dryfesdale*) 46

* The modern forms in parenthesis are partly from the other lists
and partly my own additions.

† *Of the same, i. e., Dunwoddy of Dunwoddy.*

LIDDESDALE AND DEBATEABLE LAND.

Armstrongs 300
Elwoods (*Eliots*) 74
Nixons 32

GALLOWAY.

Laird of Dawybaylie........... 41
Orcherton................................ 111
Carlisle 206
Loughenwar (*Gordon ?*).................. 45
Tutor of Bombie *........................ 140
Abbot of Newabbey 141
Town of Dumfries......................... 201
Town of Kircubrie 36

TIVIDALE.

Laird of Drumlire...... 364
Caruthers 71
Trumbells................................ 12

ESKDALE.

Battisons and Thomsons.................. 166

The following East Border chiefs did homage to the Duke of Somerset at the same time, viz. : the Lairds of Cessforth (*Ker*), Fernyherst (*Ker*), Grenehead (*Ker*), Hunthill (*Rutherford*), Hundely (*Ruth-*

---

* Bombie belonged to the Maclellans. Tutor signifies Guardian or Trustee, and they were almost invariably designed from the name of the estate put under their charge — generally when the heir was a minor.

erford), Makerstone (*MacDougal*), Warmesay
( ), Syntoun (*Lynton? Ker?*), Egerston
( ), Merton ( ), Mowe (*of that Ilk*),
Rydell (*of that Ilk*), Beamerside (*Haig*), and the
following gentlemen, viz. : George Tromboul, Jhon
Haliburton, Robert Car, Robert Car of Greyden,
Adam Kirton, Andrew Mether, Saunders Purvose
of Erleston, Mark Car of Littledean, George Car of
Faldenside, Alexander Mackdowal, Charles Ruther-
ford, Thomas Car of the Yere, Jhon Car of Meyn-
thorn (*Nenthorn*), Walter Holiburton, Richard
Hangansyde, Andrew Car, James Douglas of Cavers,
James Car of Mersington, George Hoppringle, Wil-
liam Ormeston of Emerden, John Grymslowe.

A West Border list of the contingents at the battle
of Dryfe Sands in 1593 (considered, however, a
doubtful one), mentions Crichton, Drumlanrig
(*Douglas*) and Dalziel, five score each ; Dalswinton
(*Stewart*) and Cowhill (*Maxwell*), eighty-nine each ;
Kirkpatrick, Carnsalloch (*Maxwell*) and Brecken-
side (*Maxwell*), full four score each ; Charteris,
sixty ; Lag (*Grierson*), fifty-four ; Lord Maxwell,
eight hundred, and Kirkconnel (*Maxwell*), one hundred.

There is a partial roll of the year 1587, from a
MS. of that period preserved in the records of the
privy council, of which I transcribe that part relating
to the Borders. It contains the titles only, but I
have added the surnames in parenthesis. It it entitled :

The Rolls of the Names of the Landislordis and Baillies duelland in the Borders and in the Hielandis quhair broken Men hes dwelt and presently dwellis.

BORDERS, MIDDLE MARCH.

Earle Bothuile (*Bothwell*), Laird of Phairny-hurst (*Ker*),* Earl of Angus (*Douglas*), Laird of Bukcleuch (*Scott*), Sherif of Teviotdale (*Douglas of Cavers*), Laird of Bedroule (*Turnbull*), Laird of Mynto (*Turnbull*), Laird of Wauchop (*Turnbull*), Lord Heries (*Harries, afterward Earl of Nithsdale*), Laird of Howpaislott (*Scott*), George Turneble of Halroule, Laird of Littledene (*Ker*), Laird of Drum-lanrig (*Douglas*), Laird of Chisholme (*Chisholme*), Laird of Johnnstoun (*Johnstone*), Laird of Apilgirth (*Jardine*), Laird of Holmendis (*Carruthers*), Laird of Graitnay (*Johnstone*), Lord Heries (*sic-bis*), Laird of Dynwyddie (*of that Ilk, or Maxwell*), Laird of Lochinvar (*Gordon*).

There is another list of the same period in the privy council records of only eighteen names, all of which are recorded in these lists except only " Moff-ettis " and " Latimers."

The following is that part relating to the Borders, of the commencement and all but completion of an

---

* " The Kers were aye the deadliest foes
That e'er to Englishmen were known,
For they were all bred left-handed men,
And fence against them there was none."

The Raid of the Kers. By the Ettrick Shepherd.

intended roll of the names of the landed proprietors
over the whole of Scotland in 1590, from the records
of the privy council. I have again added the surnames to the best of my ability in parenthesis. It
is entitled:

The Roll of the Clannis that hes Capitanis,
Cheiffis,* Chiftenis, quhomeon they depend, oftymis
aganis the willis of thair Landislordis, alsweill on
the Bordouris as Hielandis, and of sum special personis of branches of the saidis Clannis.

Landit Men.

BERUIK. Lord Hume (*or Home*), Woddirburne
(*Home*), Coldounknowis (*Home*), Aytoun (*Home*),
Polwart (*Home*), Manderstoun (*Home*), Hutounhall
(*Home*), Blacater (*Home*), David Hume of the Law,
Nynewellis (*Home*), Hume of Eist Restoun, Billie
(*Renton*), Blanerne (*Lumsden*), Cumlitche (*Affleck*),
Slychthoussis (*Sleich*), Hoprig (*Lyle*), Rentoun
(*Home*), Craw in Gunnisgrene, Swyntoun (*of that
Ilk*), Lanfurmacus (*Sinclair*), Cockburn (*of that Ilk*),
Langtoun (*Cockburn*), Butterden (*Ellem or Ellam*),
Grenelaw (*Home*), Reidpeth (*Redpath*), Eist Nysbet
(*Chirnside*), West Nisbet (*Ker*), Restalrig (*Ker*),
Eddrem (   ), Wyliecleuch (*Ramsay*), Spottis-
wood (*of that Ilk*), Woddirlie (*Edgar*), Thornydikes
(*Brown*), Corsbye (*Crossby of that Ilk, or Home*),

---

* In the Highlands the three pinion feathers of the eagle was the
distinguishing badge of a chief, two of a chieftain and one of a
gentleman. This mark of nobility was as old as the time of Ossian.

Goodman of Moreistoun (*Ker*), Greinlawdene (*Bromfield*), Pittilisheuch (*Bromfield**), Hardaikers (*Bromfield*), Eistfield (*Bromfield*), Todrig (*Bromfield*), Mellertoun (   ), Lambden (*Haitlie*), Buchtrig (*Dickson*), Belchester (*Dickson*), Lithame (*Dickson*), Peill (*Dickson*), Heirdrig (*Dickson*), Edingtoun (*Ramsay*), Mersingtoun (*Ker, previously Dickson*), W. Hume of Bassinden, Guidman of Growadykis (*Duns?*), Guidman of Chowislie (*Cockburn*), Burnehoussie (*Pringle*), Lard Purves in Ersiltoun, St. Johnischapell (*Baillie*), Lauder (*of that Ilk*), Bowmaker, Prentonen (*Trotter*).

ANNANDERDAILL. Johnnstoun (*of that Ilk*), Apilgirth (*Jardine*), Holmendis (*Carruthers*), Corheid (*Johnstone*), Frenscheland (*French*), Bodisbeik (*Hewitt?*), Wamphray (*Johnstone*), Dynwoddie (*of that Ilk, or Jardine or Maxwell?*), Elscheschelis (*Johnstone*), Halathis (   ), Cokpule (*Murray*), Nubye (*Johnstone*), Wormombye (*Irving*), Corrie (*Johnstone*), Castelmylk (*Stewart or Maxwell*), Boneschaw (*Irving*), Brydekirk-Carlile (*Carlyle of Bridekirk*), Locarby (*Johnstone*), Purdoun (*Purdon of Glendenning?*), Glencors (*of that Ilk*), Reidkirk (*Graham*), Blawatwod (*Graham*), Gillisbye (*Graham*), Wauchop-Lindsay.

ROXBURGH AND SELKIRK. Cesfurd (*Ker*), Greneheid (*Ker*), Littleden (*Ker*), Sir John Ker of Hirsell, Fawdounsyde (*Ker*), Gaitschaw (*Ker*), Corbett (*Ker*), Garden (*Gradon-Ker?*), Schaw of

---

* In 1607 it belonged to a Dickson.

Dalcoif, Quhitmore (*Whitmore*), Quhitmurehall (*Ker*), Sunderlandhall (*Ker*), Lyntoun (*Ker*), Yair (*Ker*), Phairnyhurst (*Ker*), Ancrum (*Ker*), Robene Ker of Newtoun, Andro Ker of Newhall, Thomas Ker of Caveris, Wat Ker of Lochtour, Andro Ker of Hietoun, James Ker of Lyntellie, Mackerstoun (*Macdougal*), Steidrig (*McDowell of Stodrig*), Mow (*of that Ilk*), Riddell (*of that Ilk*), Edmestoun (*Edmondstone*), Mungo Bennet of Chesteris, William Kirktoun of Stewartfield, William Anislie of Fawlay, Overtoun (*Fraser*), William Mader of Langtoun, Hundeley (*Rutherford*), Hunthill (*Rutherford*), Edzarstoun (*Rutherford*), George Rutherfud of Fairnyngtoun, David Rutherfurd of the Grange, Johne Rutherfurde in the Toftis, Johnne Rutherfurd of the Knowe in Nysbit, William Rutherfurd in Littleheuch, Walter Turneble in Bedroule, John Turneble of Mynto, Hector Turnble of Wauchop, Turnble of Halroule, George Turnble of the Toftis, Hector Turnble of Bernehillis, Walter Turnble of Bewlye, Turnble of Belses, James Turneble of the Tour, Turnble of Bullerwall, Edward Lorane of Harwood, James Douglas of Caveris, sheriff, William Douglas of Bonejedburgh, Tympenden (*Douglas*), Johnne Douglas of Quhitrig, Gavin Ellot of Stobbis, Well Ellot of Harthscarth, tutour of Reidheuch, Will Ellot of Fallinesche, Robin Ellot of Braidley, Mangertoun (*Armstrong*), Quhittauch (*Armstrong*), Bukcleuch (*Scot*), Wat Scot of Goldelandis, Robert Scott of

12

Allanhauch, Howpaislott (*Scot*), Glak (*Elphinstone*), Eidschaw (*Scot*), Syntoun (*Scot*), Lard of Hassinden (   ), Walt Scott of Chalmerlane, Newtoun (*Scot ?*), Guidman of Burnefute (*Scot ?*), Wat Scott of Stirkschawis, Robert Scott of Thirlstane, James Scott of Robertoun, Wat Scott of Harden, Mr. Arthur Scott of Wynterburgh, Michael Scott of Aikwood, Will Scott of Hartwodmyris, Robert Scott of Hanyng, Adam Scott of Bonyngtoun, Wat Scot of Tuschelaw, Will Scott of Montbergner, Philip Scott of Dryhoip, Will Scott of Huntlie, Gledstanis (*Gladstone*), Langlandis (*of that Ilk*), Chesholm (*of that Ilk*), Ailmure (*Armstrong*), Walter Vaitche of Northsyntoun, Patrick Murray of Fawlayhill, Thom Dalgleische of Deuchar, Gallowscheilis* (*Pringle*), Quhitebank (*Pringle*), Bukholme (*Pringle*), Torwodley (*Pringle*), Blindley (*Pringle*), Trinlingknowis (*Pringle*), Newhall (*Pringle*), Torsons (*Pringle*), Murehous Pryingle).

PEBLIS. Traquair (*Stewart*), Blakbarony (*Murray*), Drummelyair (*Tweedie*), Scraling (*Cockburn*), Pyrne (*Cranstoun*), Smythfield (*Haye, anciently Dickson*), Maner (*Lowis*), Manerheid (*Inglis*), Posso (*Nasmyth*), Dawick (*Veitch*), Dreva (   ), Charles Geddes of Rachane, Polmude (*Hay*), Halkschaw (*Douglas ?*), Furd (*Froude*), Erlhauch (   ), Barnis (*Burnet ?*), Caverhill (   ), Fowletche (*Stewart*), Myl-

---

* Galashiels. Not derived from a gallows-tree, but from the Celtic *gea lia*, *i. e.*, sorcery stone, a name sometimes given to Druidical remains.

comstoun-Pringle, William Tuedy of the Wra, Robert Creichtoun of the Quarter, Romannois (*Penicuik*), Quothquot ( ), Stanypeth-Douglas, James Lausoun of Carnemiur, Sandelandis of Boyle, Purveshill (*Laverokstane*), Hartrie (*Brown*), Mitchellhill ( ), Langlandhill (*Inglis*), Glen (*Bar*), Erlisochert (*Lindsay*), Cowrehoip ( ).

DUMFRIES. Drumlanrig (*Douglas*), Macmath (*of that Ilk*), Achingassil (*Maitland*), Achinsell (*Menzies*), Closburn (*Kirkpatrick*), Kirkmichael ( ), Amysfield (*Charteris*), Tynewall (*Maxwell*), Lag (*Grierson*), Schawis (*Ker?*), Craigdarroch (*Ferguson*), Bardannoch (*Pringle*), Cloglyne ( ), Glenislein (*Kirks*), Sundeywall ( ), Freir-Kers (*Kerse of Frier*), Conhaith (*Maxwell*), Kirkconnel (*Maxwell. There were also both Gordons and Irvings of Kirkconnel*), Carnesalloch (*Maxwell*), Spottis (*Hume*), Tarrachtie ( ), Eglisfechan (*Carruthers*), Partoun (*Glendenning*), Almygill (*MacBrair*), Robgill (*Irving*), Hoilhouse (*Armstrong*), Linclouden ( ), Coschogill (*Douglas*), Dalvene (*Douglas*), Castelhill (*Menzies*), Erll Mortoun, Lord Sanquhar, Lord Maxwell, Lord Hereis.

Although official this roll is not perfect. Dickson of Ormeston, Co. Peebles is omitted, but the family were seated there as early at least as 1390–1406, and twelve years later than the date of this list Dickson of Ormeston signed a Band to the King.

A Band or Bond, dated August 6, 1591, preserved in Rymer's Foedera, contains the names of several

Barons and Gentlemen of the Eastern Marches who pledged themselves faithfully to serve the King against Earl Bothwell. It was signed by "Cesford (*Ker**), Minto (*Turnbull*), Hundley (*Earl of*) Wat of Badroul (*Walter Turnbull of Bedrule*), Jedburgh (*Provost of*), Harlwood (*Inglis?*) Wedderburne (*Home*), Huttonhall (*Home*), Alexander Hume of Northberick, Maynes Ayton younger (*Hume, Jr. of Ayton*), James Bronfield for the surname of the Bronfields, John Readpith, Patrick Dixson, Blacader younger (*Home Jr. of Blackadde*), East (*Home*), Nisbet (*of that Ilk*), Innerwick (*of that Ilk*), Swinton (*of that Ilk*), Baylie (*of St. John's Chapel*), Renton (*of Billie?*), Pranderguest (*Horne*), Andro Car (*Ker*) of Fawside, Saltcoats (*Livingstone*), Hermiston (   ), and as Rymer adds, "With sundry others."

Another Band to be found in the Records of the Privy Council was signed at Edinburgh the same day, and to the same effect, as follows :—

"The subscribers faithfully promise to serve and obey the King, his lieutenants and wardens in all things tending to the advancement and forthsetting of his majesty's authority, and in particular in the pursuit of Francis, sometime Earl Bothwill, Alexander, Lord Hume and other declared traitors, their assistors, resetters and intercommuners. Should any of the said rebels come within the bounds or lands of the said subscribers they will apprehend them if

---

* Surnames in italics added by the author.

they can 'or utherwayis sall schowte and rais the fray' with their whole forces and join with others against them * * * under the penalty of 10,000 merks each."

Subscribed at Edinburgh this 6th August, 1591, by "Cessfurde (*Ker*), Bukcleugh (*Scot*), Johnne Edmonstoun, G. Houm of Broxmouth, G. Lauder of Bas, Andro Ker of Lyntoun, James Douglas of Cavers, David Rentowne of Billie, Alexander Diksoun, George Trottar of Keirtoun, J. Reidpeth, William Reidpeth, Johnne Graden, William Furd, Johnne Rutherfurd, * * * of West Neisbit, Watt Turnbull of Bedroule, Johnne Turnbull of Mynto, Hector Turnbull of Wauchope, Robert Diksoun of Buchtrig, Andro Diksoun of Belchester, George Haitlie in Hordlaw and John Graden of Ernislaw."

Ridpath in his Border History says of the first of these two Bonds that it was signed by " Most of the *considerable* barons and gentlemen."

Five signed both bonds but with the customary carelessness spelt their names differently in the two documents.

Of the forty-one signers whose names have been preserved four were Dicksons.

In concluding this brief sketch I now copy Moni: penny's List of the Border Clans in 1597, from the edition of 1603, reprinted by Baron Somers (London, 1809), as the list which is especially interesting to Genealogists is omitted in the later editions of that scarce little tract, which is of trifling value otherwise, the remainder being merely an abbreviation of Hector Boece, the most untrustworthy of Scottish Historians.

The Names of the principall Clannes and Surnames of the Borders, not landed, and Chiefe Men of Name amongst them at this present. A. D. 1597.

[This heading is evidently incorrect, as in the preceding Government Roll of 1590 many of the following names occur under "Landed Men." The title should be " landed, and not landed," for those styled " of " were landowners, and those called " in " were tenants, but still chief men of name. As, for instance, William Trotter *of* Foulschawe was a landlord, while Cuthbert Trotter *in* Fogo, although a leading man, was not.

While the eldest son was styled " younger of," the term *in* seems sometimes to have been given to the younger members of the family. John Dickson *de* Belchester is mentioned in 1539, but in 1603 we meet with a John Dickson *in* Belchester.]

East March.

Brumfields.

John Brumfield, tutor of Greynelawdene, Adam Brumfield of Hardaikers, Brumfield of Pittilisheuch, Alexander Brumfield of Eastfield, Alexander Brumfield of Hasilton Maynes, James Brumfield of Whytehouse, the Laird of Todderike, Alexander Brumfield of Gordon Maines.

Trotter.

The Laird of Pentennen, William Trotter of Foulschawe, Cuthbert Trotter in Fogo, Tome Trotter of the Hill.

Diksons.

The goodman of Buchtrig,* The goodman of Bolchester, Dikson of Hassington, Dikson in Newbigging.

Ridpaths.

Thomas Ridpath of Crumrig, Alexander Ridpath of Angelraw.

Haitlies.

The goodman of Lambden, John Haitlie of Brumehill, George Haitlie in Hardlaw, Lawrence Haitlie in Haliburton.

Gradenis.

Jasper Graden in Ernislaw.

Young.

James Young of the Criffe, Will Young of Otterburne, David Young of Oxemsyde, William Scott of Feltershawes.

---

* This is an error, as both Buhtrig and Belchester were *tenants in capite,* or crown vassals holding charters from the king. The distinction formerly recognized was that the laird was a crown vassal or baron; the gudeman, one who held his lands from a baron, and when, in place of military service, a return was made in grain or in money, he was sometimes called a feuar.

Davisons.

Roben Davison of Symeston, Jok Davison of Quhitton, James Davison of Byrnirig, George Davison of Throgdan.

Pringils.

James Hoppringill of Towner, Walt Hoppringill of Clifton, John Hoppringill of the Bents, David Hoppringill of Morbottle.

Tates.

Will Tate in Stankfurde, David Tate in Cheritries, David Tate in Bair-ers, Will Tate in Zettane.

Middelmaists.

Robin Middilemaist in Milrig.

Burnes.

David Burne of Ellisheuch, Ralph Burne of the Coit.

Daglesches.

Jok Dagleisch of Bank, Robert Dagleisch in Wide-open.

Gilchristis.

Hugh Gilchrists called of Cowbene, Will Gilchrist in Cavertoun.

Hall.

John Hall of Newbigging, George Hall called Pats Geordie there, Andrew Hall of the Sykes, Thom Hall in Fowlscheils.

Pyle.

George Pyle in Milkheuch, John Pyle in Swynsyde.

Robeson.

Ralph Robeson in Prenderlech, Rinzean Robeson in Howston.

Anislie.

William Anislie of Fawlaw, Lancie Anislie in Oxnem.

Oliver.

David Oliver in Hynhanchheid, Will Oliver in Lustruther, George Oliver in Clarely.

Laidlow.

Ryne Laidlow in the Bank, John Laidlow in Sonnysyde.

LIDDESDAIL.

The Laird of Mangerton (*Armstrong**), The Lairds Jok (*Armstrong*), Chrystie of the Syde (*Armstrong*).

Quhithauch.

The Laird of Quhithauch (*Armstrong*), Johnie of Quhithauch (*Armstrong*), Sym of the Maynes (*Armstrong*).

---

* Mangerton was the chief of the Armstrongs. The famous Gilnochie was a son of this house. The Laird's Jok signifies The Laird's son Jok.

The names in parenthesis are my own addition.

13

Merietown Quarter.

Archie of Westburnflat (*Armstrong*), Wanton Sym in Quhitley Syde (*Armstrong*), Will of Powderlanpat (*Armstrong*).

Ellots.

Redheuch,* Robert Ellot and Martyne Ellot.

Thoirlishop.

Rob of Thoirlishop, Arthur fyre the Brays (*Eliot*).

Gorumberie.

Archie Keene, Wil of Morspatrikshors (*Eliot*).

Parke.

Johnne of the Park, Gray Wil.

Burnheid.

Gawins Jok, Ade Cowdais.

Welschaw.

Wil Colichis Hob, Hob of Bowholmes.

Niksons.

John Nikson of Laiest burne, Georgies Harie Nikson, Cleme Nikson, called the Crune.

Crosers.

Hob Croser called Hob of Ricarton, Martin Croser, Cokkis John Croser, Noble Clemeis Croser.

---

* The Laird of Larriston was the chief rider of the Eliots, who were often called Elwoods and Elwands.

Hendersons.

Rinzian Henderson in Armiltonburne, Jenkyne Henderson in Kartley.

DEBAITABLE LAND.

Sandeis Barnes Armestrangs.

Will of Kinmouth, Krystie Armestrang, John Skynbanke.

Lardis Rinzians Gang.

Lairdis Rinziane,* Lairdis Robbie, Rinzian of Wauchop.

Grahams.

Priors, John and his Bairnes, Hector of the Harlaw, The griefs and cuts of Harlaw.

EWISDAILL.

Armestrangs of the Gyngils.

Ekke of the Gyngils, Andrew of the Gyngils, Thome of Glendoning.

Scotts.

Thome of the Flower, Anfe of the Busse.

Ellots.

John the Portars sonne, Will of Devisleyes, Wil the lord.

ESKDAILL.

Battisons of Cowghorlae.

David Batie, Hugh Batie, Mungoes Arthurie, Adame of the Burne.

---

* Rinzian is the common pronunciation of Ninian.

Batisons of the Scheill.

Nichol of the Scheill, Androw of Zetbyre, John the Braid, Wat of the Corse.

Johnes.

John Armstrang of Hoilhous, John Armstrang of Thornequhat, Wil Armstrang of Ternsnihil.

Littils.

John Littill of Casshoke, Thome Littill of Finglen, Ingrahames Archie Littill.

ANANDAILL.

Irwingis.

Edward of Bonschaw, Lang Richies Edward, John the young Duke, Chrystie Cothquhat, Willie of Graitnayhill.

Bellis.

Will Bell of Alby, John Bell of the Tourne, Mathie Bell called the King, Andro Bell called Lokkis Andro, Will Bell Reidcloke.

Carlilles.

Adam Carlile of Bridekerk, Alexander Carlile of Egleforhame.

Grahams.

George Grahame of Reupatrik, Arthour Grahame of Blawoldwood, Richie Grahame called the Plump.

Thompsons.

Young Archie Thomson, Sym Thomson in Polloden.

Romes.

Roger Rome in Tordoweth, Mekle Sandie Rome there.

Gasses.

David Gasse in Barch, John Gasse Michael's sonne in Rig.

Monipenny says the last twenty-one, viz. : the Irvings, Bells, Carlisles, Grahams, Thomsons, Romes and Gasses, were "Chief men of name not being lairds."

The list is imperfect, and perhaps it was for that reason it was omitted in the later editions. The author has not even mentioned the Homes, Kers, Johnstones, Turnbulls and others, and has hardly named the Scotts. Under Liddesdale the surnames of the first-named families are not given, but the Eliots and Grahams appear twice, the Armstrongs oftener, and in one place they are classed under the Johnes, and the Beatties are called both Baties and Battisons.

They were fond of to-names, which were in fact necessary for distinction when there were so few baptismal names scattered through a clan, and some of the *sobriquets* are peculiar. An Eliot of Thorles-hope is styled Arthur Fire-the-braes. Braes generally signify hills or the upper part of the country, as the Braes of Angus. Did he fire the braes as the North American Indians fire the prairies ? Another Eliot is called the porter's son. One Bell is called

the King and another Redcloak; but what does the
name of a Graham signify, "The griefs and cuts of
Harlaw?"

In the records of the privy council I find a Gib
Elliot called Sweet Milk, another Elliot called the
Cleg (*gadfly*), and a third Cauldfute (*cold foot*); an
Armstrong is styled Bonybutis (*pretty boots*). Hob
Johnstone is called Goode at Even (*Good in the
evening*); Wil Scot, Stand in the rain; Jok Scot,
As-it-Luikis (*As it looks*); John Innes Garmouth
callit the Sweet Man, and John Adam callit Meat
and Rest!

Monipenny gives another list, of which I only
copy that part referring to the Borders. It is as
follows:

The Names of the Barons, Lairds and chiefe Gentlemen in every Sherifdome.

As they were Anno Domini, 1597.

Berwike and Lawderdaill.

L. of Wedderburne, Home. L. of Blacatour,
Home. L. of Aytoun, Home. L. of Coldenknowes,
Home. L. of Polwart, Home. Hume of Manderstoun, Home. L. of Hutonhall, Home. L. of Langton [*Cockburn*].* L. of Billie [*Renton*]. L. of Blanerne

---

* The names in brackets were added by Baron Somers, those in
parenthesis by myself; but sometimes lairdships changed lands,
and again it occasionally happened that there were more places
than one of the same name. There was more than one Newbigging
(New house), and probably more than one Nubie or Newby (New
dwelling), and at least three Ormistons. In such cases it is not
always certain which is the one referred to.

[*Lumsden*]. L. of Cumletche, Aflek (*Affleck*). L. of
Edingtoun [*Ramsay*]. Slychthous (*Sleich*). Butter-
dayne (*Ellem or Ellame ?*). Hoprig (*Lyle*). East
Nisbet (*Chirnside*). West Nisbet [*Ker*]. Wedderlie
[*Edgar*]. Thorniedykes [*Browne*]. L. of Spottiswood
[*of that Ilk*]. Cranstoun of Thirlstane-maines. Cors-
bie (*Crossby of that Ilk*, or *Home ?*). Bemersyde
[*Haig*]. Mertoun [*Haliburton*]. L. Swyntoun [*Swin-
ton*]. L. Redpeth [*Ridpath*]. Greenlaw [*Home*].
Lochurmachus [*Sinclair*]. L. Glammilscheilis, Home.
Wylielewcht (*Ramsay*).

Roxburgh.

L. of Cesfurde, Ker. L. of Litledane, Ker. L. of
Greynhede, Ker. L. of Corbet, Ker. Gradon, Ker.
Ker of Gaitschaw. Mow [*Mow or Molle*] (*of that Ilk*).
Haddon [*Murray*]. Sheriffe of Teviotdaill, Dowg-
lasse. Tymperden, Douglas. Hundeley [*Ruther-
ford*]. Hunthill [*Rutherford*]. Edzarstoun [*Ruther-
ford*]. Bedreull, Turne-bull. Mynto [Stewart].*
Wawchop [*Turnbull*]. William Turnebull of Barn-
hills. George Turnebull of Halreull. Hector Lorane
of Harwood. Grinyslaw of little Norton. Mader of
Langton. Mungo Bennet of Chestis. Overtoun,
Frasier. Riddale of that Ilk. L. Makkayrstoun
(*Makdowgal*). Andrew Ker of Fadounsyde. L. of
Bakeleuch, Scot. Raph Haliburton of Mourhouslaw.

---

* In 1329 the lands of Mynto belonged to Walter Turnbull, but in
the time of Robert III (1390–1406) they were divided between the
Turnbulls and the Stewarts, who both possessed them until about
1622, when they again changed hands.

Thomas Ker of Cavers. Howpasloth, Scott. Baron
Gledstanes [*Gladstone*]. Langlands [*Langlands*].
William Ellot of Torslyhill. Scott of Sintoun. Scott
of Eydschaw. Walter Vaitch of Northsintoun. Scott
of Glæke. L. of Chesholme of that Ilk. L. of Cranstoun (*Cranstown*). Kirktoun of Stewartfield. L. of
Linton, Ker. Ker of Ancrum. Carncors of Colmislie.

*Dumfries with the Stewartries of Kirkcudbright
and Anandail.*

L. of Lochin-war, Gordon. L. of Troquhayre,
Gordon. L. of Barskeoche, Gordon. L. of Airdis,
Gordon. Sheirmæs, Gordon. Gordon of the Cule.
L. of Broughton, Murray. L. of Dalbatie (*Reddik,
Rodyk or Rerik*). L. of Portoun, Glendoning. L. of
Bomby (*Maclellan*). Maclellane of Mærtoun. L. of
Cardenes (*Macculloch*). Lidderdaill of S. Mary Ile.
Lindesay of Barcloy. Heries of Madinhoip. L. of
Mabie, Hereis. Macknaught of Kilquhanatie. Glen-
duynning of Drumrasche. Maxwell of the Hill. Sin-
clair of Auchinfranke. Maxwell of the Logane. Max-
well of Dromcoltrane. Stewart of Fintillauche.
Levinston of Little Ardis. L. of Drumlanrig, Dowg-
lasse. Dowglasse of Caskogill. Creichtoun of Carco.
Creichtoun of Liberie. Macmath of that Ilk. Dowg-
lasse of Dalvene. Menzies of Castelhill. Menzies of
Auchinsell. L. of Auchingassill, Maitland. L. of
Closeburne, Kirk Patrik. Kirkmichael. Goodman of
Frier, Kerse. L. of Lag, Grier (*Grierson*). L. of
Amysfield, Charteris. Maxwell of Gowhill. Maxwell

of Porterrake. Maxwell of Tynwald. Maxwell of Con-
haith. Maxwell of Carnsallauch. Maxwell of the Ile.
Browne of the Lawne. Cunningham of Kirkschaw.
L. of Craigdarroch (*Ferguson*). L. of Bardannoch
(*Pringle?*). Kirko of Glenesslane. Ballagane (*Hun-
ter?*). L. of Johnestown (*Johnstone*). L. of Wamfra,
Johnestone. L. of Eschescheilis (*Johnstone*). L. of
Corheid, Johnstone. L. of Corry (*Johnstone*). L. of
Newbie, Johnstone. L. of Graitnay, Johnestone.
Johnstone of Craighop-burne. Johnestone of New-
tone. Johnstone of Kirkton. L. of Apilgirth, Jarden.
L. of Holmends (*Carruthers*). L. of Cockpoole,
Murray. L. of Moryquhat (*Murray of Murray-
thwaite*). L. of Wormondby (*Irving*). L. of Knok
(*Knox?*). Goodman of Granton (*Melville or Gor-
don?*). Boidisbyke (*Hewitt?*).

Peiblis.

The Knight of Traquair, Stewart. L. of Pyrn,
Cranstoun. L. of Horsburgh [*Horsburgh*]. L. of
Greistown (*Middelmaist?*). L. of Cardono [*William-
son*]. L. of Henderstown (*Ephinstone*). L. of Smeyth-
field [*Haye*] (*anciently Dickson*). L. of Winkiston
[*Twedie*] (*anciently Dickson*). L. of Blackbarrony,
Murray. Bernys [*Burnet*]. Caverhill. Fowllœche,
Stewart. L. of Drummelzear, Twedie. Dawik [*Veitch*],
Pobinde [*Hunter*]. Frude (*Froude*). Halkshaw
(*Douglas?*). Glengirk (*Porteous of Glenkirk*). Geddes
of Rachane. Inglis of Langlandhill. L. of Straling,
Hartrie (*Brown, afterward Dickson*). Romannos
14

[*Pennicuik*]. Prettishoil. Meluingshland (*anciently Dickson*). Ormestoun (*Dickson*). Bonytoun (*Wooa*). Posso, Nasmyth. John Hamilton of Coltcote.

Entire dependence cannot be placed upon this list, as among the Highland Clans I find Monipenny calls the then Lord Lovat John, while on the contrary his name was Hugh. It appears to be an appendix to his first list, but still imperfect.

Some Scottish families have been described with reference to the qualities of their more conspicuous members. I am indebted principally to Dr. Rogers (*Traits and Stories of the Scottish People*), for the following list in alphabetical order, but must confess to having omitted a few, which, to say the least, were not complimentary.

The sturdy Armstrongs.
The trusty Boyds.*
The famous Dicksons.
The lucky Duffs.
The bauld (bold) Frasers.
The gay Gordons.
The gallant Grahams.
The haughty Hamiltons.
The handsome Hays.
The haughty Humes.
The jingling Jardines.
The gentle Johnstones.†

---

* So called by Blind Harry five centuries ago.

† This must have been ironical.

The angry Kerrs.
The light Lindsays.*
The brave Macdonalds.
The fiery Mackintoshes.
The proud Macneils.
The black Macreas.
The wild Macraws.
The manly Morrisons.
The muckle mou'ed Murrays.†
The gentle Neilsons.
The bauld Rutherfords.
The saucy Scotts.
The proud Setons.‡
The pudding Somervilles.§
The worthy Watsons.

Not only Borderers but also Highlanders and Lowlanders are included in the above. The latter were the inhabitants of Fife and the Lothians, which were situated between the two others. The Douglasses had two appellations : the house of Angus was characterized as The red Douglas ; that of Liddesdale as The black Douglas.

---

* "The Lindsays *light and gay.*"

† The origin of this appellation is too well known to be repeated.

‡ Or tall and proud as the Setons.

§ From a king's joke. King James V was often entertained at the hospitable board of Lord Somerville and told him he ought to carry a pudding in his coat of arms.

The Border Clans were broken up about the time
of the Union of the Crowns, A. D. 1603, when the
King prohibited the name of the Borders any longer
to be used, substituting in its place those of middle
shires.   He also ordered all the places of strength
to be demolished except the habitations of noblemen
and barons, their iron gates to be converted into
plough-shares, and the inhabitants to betake themselves to agriculture and other works of peace.

Peace did not immediately follow however.   In
1609 the Earl of Dunbar informs the King that he
had cut off "the Laird of of Tynwald, Maxwell, sundry Douglasses, Johnstones, Jardines, Armstrongs,
Beatisons and sic others, *magni nominis luces* in that
broken parts," and thereby rendered that part of the
kingdom peaceable.   In 1618 a hundred and twenty
men of the Borders were apprehended by the landlords and wardens of the Middle Marches and sent
to the Bohemian Wars, and as late as 1637, a commission headed by the Earl of Traquair sat at Jedburgh, when a great number were branded, fined or
banished, and thirty were hanged.

But highwaymen plied their trade in the suburbs
of the very city of London itself long after the
Borders were comparatively secure.

INDEX OF DICKSON LANDED TITLES.

TENANTS.

THE CLAN DICKSON.

Like all surnames the name of this clan has been variously written at different periods.

In a charter from King Robert Bruce, about A. D. 1306, to Thomas Dicson, it occurs as filius Ricardi (*son of Richard*), and the charter is indorsed "Carta Thome fil Dick."

It has also been written:

Decksoune.	Dickesoun.	Dikkesone.
Dekonsoun.	Dickiesoune.	Dikkonsone.
Dekysoun.	Dickesone.	Dikonsoun.
Dykisoun.	Dikesoun.	Dikson.
Dykysoun.	Dikesone.	Diksone.
Dykkyson.	Dikeson.	Diksoune.
Dyckison.	Dikison.	Diksoun.
Dycson.	Dikisoune.	Dixson.
Dykson.	Dikysoun.	Dixon.
Dyxcoun.	Dikconsoune.	Dickson.
Dicson.		

Perhaps also Diksame, for in a list of Scottish Noblemen and Gentlemen taken prisoners at the battle of Solway Moss in 1542, occurs the name John Diksame, who was probably a Dickson.

15

These variations of spelling proper names are not peculiar to Scotland. I think it was Dugdale who stated that he had found over one hundred and forty variations of the name of Mainwaring or Mannering, anciently de Mesnilwarin.

Dickson is now the usual form in Scotland, but in England where the similar name is not a clan name, and where there are numerous different families who do not pretend to claim a common origin, but all derive their surname from being sons of various Dicks, it is almost invariably written Dixon.

The clan are descended from the Keiths, Earls Marshall, one of the most powerful families in Scotland, when, with the sole exception of the Royal Family, the title of Earl was the highest in the kingdom, and who had so many possessions that it was formerly said that they could journey from the north to the south of Scotland and sleep every night in one of their own castles.

This descent is proved by no less than three entries in the Records of the Lyon Office between the years 1672 and 1694.

And here it may be well to explain that during a temporary occupation of the country by the English most of the public records, including those of the Lyon Office, were shipped to London and lost at sea, and about the year 1670, the remaining records of that office were destroyed by fire.

The earliest Register of Arms, now extant, is that of Sir David Lindsay, Lord Lyon King at Arms, containing over three hundred shields beautifully emblazoned, with the names added, as "Dikesoun of yat Ilk." This which was executed about 1542, was authenticated by the Scottish Privy Council in 1630, and is preserved in the Advocate's library.

In 1672, an act of Parliament was made ordaining all the nobility and gentry to register their armorial bearings, but Nisbet complains that many of the most ancient and considerable families neglected to register, partly through indolence and partly through a false pride, considering themselves so well known that it was unnecessary.

Three of our name obeyed the law, the first of whom is entered thus: "Mr.* Robert Dickson, Advocat, descended of yᵉ familie of yᵉ Earle Marischall, Bears," — etc. The second reads: "Mr. Alexander Dicksone of Westerbinning, descended of the family of Buhtrig which was descended of the Earle Marshall, Bears,"— etc., and the third is as follows: "Captain Robert Dickson of Sornbeg, and which surname was originally Keith, Bears,"— etc.

Nisbet in his Heraldry (Edinburgh, 1722) says the Dicksons are descended from one Richard Keith, said to be a son of the family of Keiths Earls Marshall of Scotland, and in proof thereof carry in their arms the chief of Keith Marischal.

This Richard was commonly called Dick, and his sons were styled after him, the affix of son in the

---

Lowlands answering to the prefix of Mac in the Highlands.

It is probable that he was the son of the Great Marshal Hervey de Keth, who died in 1249, by his wife Margaret, daughter of William third Lord Douglas, because it was customary in Scotland in those days before the introduction of quartering for cadets to compose their Arms by adding to their paternal bearing a part or the whole of their mother's Arms to show their maternal descent, and to difference themselves from other descendants of the family, and the Arms of Keith are Argent on a Chief gules three pallets or (but Nisbet says in several paintings the chief is paly of six or and gules, which agrees with their traditionary origin that at a battle with the Danes a chief of the Keith's slew the Danish leader, which being perceived by King Malcolm, he drew, with the blood of the dead man, long stripes on the conqueror's shield — and also agrees with the Chief of Dickson of Buhtrig), while the House of Douglas, before the death of the Bruce in 1329, bore simply Azure three mullets argent. The heart was added by William first Earl of Douglas, and appears on his seal in 1343.

Some of the Dicksons seem to have preferred the Douglas mullets alone, for Thomas (II) of Hazelside, who succeeded his father in 1307, bore a sword between two mullets, and others bore mullets only.

The Dicksons of Buhtrig, however, bore the Chief of Keith with the Douglas mullets in base, a perfect specimen of composed Arms. The early records being lost it is impossible to say when they first bore that coat, although it may have been adopted as early as when Thomas (II) of Hazelside chose his armorial bearings. They were generally assumed in those days. The granting of Arms by Herald's Colleges is of later date.

The first Dickson on record, moreover, was evidently a person of very good standing, such as a grandson of the Earl Marshall might be expected to be, a man of wealth as well as of influence, and was also a clansman of the Douglas. Two of the oldest Scottish Historians recount his deeds, Archdeacon Barbour who wrote in 1375, and Blind Harry, or Henry the Minstrel, whose metrical history was written about 1381.

There are some who speak slightingly of the bard, but Major, who was born in 1405, says he was living about that time and that he recited his compositions in the presence of princes or men of the highest rank (*coram principibus*), and Chalmers in his Caledonia, says "Blind Harrie, whom the Scotch Historians generally follow but dare not quote. Blind Harrie is, however, supported by the Tower Records."

According to the Minstrel, when Douglas wished to recover his castle of Sanquhar in 1295, he applied to Thom Dycson who was "born to himself," *i. e.*, relation or clansman by birth, and addresses him as "Dear Friend," and relied so much upon him that he afterward selected him to pass through the enemy's camp of some three thousand men to bear a message to Wallace; while Barbour says he was rich in moveables and cattle and had many friends, besides which his house could not have been a small one as it contained a private chamber where he not only concealed Douglas but also brought persons to see him without attracting notice, and the space for such a secret apartment could not have been taken out of a small house without being perceived.

It is necessary to make this explanation because Hume of Godscroft, in 1648, calls him a "servant," by which he evidently meant a feudal retainer, and Scott follows Hume without explaining the modern meaning of the word as he should have done, so that probably every reader of Castle Dangerous considers Doughty Dickson, as he is still called, to have been a menial, instead of which he was, Laird of at least two Baronies and Governor of Douglas Castle. McDowell, in his History of Dumfriesshire, absurdly styles him "a soldier of humble rank," instead of which he was a "tenant in capite," holding direct from the Crown.   This

THOMAS DICSON,

Laird of Symonston and Hesleside, county Lanark, and Castellan of Douglas, son of Dick de Keth, was born A. D. 1247, and if grandson of the aforesaid Hervey de Keth was then also second cousin to William seventh Lord Douglas, father of the good

Sir James eighth Lord, to both of whom Dickson was certainly a trusty friend.

After the capture of Berwick in 1295, Sir William Douglas wished to recover his castle of Sanquhar, then held by the English who had laid waste all the surrounding country, and accordingly as the Minstrel says, went to

> "A young man than that hardy was and bauld (*bold*),
> Born till him selff and Thom Dycson was cauld;
> Der freynd he said I wald preyff (*prove*) at my mycht,
> And mak a fray to fals Bewfurd the knycht,
> In Sanquhar duellys and dois full gret owtrage
> Than Dycson said my self in that wiage (*voyage*),
> Sall for you pass with Anderson to spek."

Anderson supplied the castle daily with fuel and Dickson persuaded him to lend him his apparel and cart. At night Douglas with thirty men concealed himself in a ravine near the castle and

> "To the Sanquhar Dickson alone he send,
> And he soon made with Anderson this end —
> Dickson should take both his horse and his weed (*dress*),
> By it was day a draught of wood to lead,
> Again he passed and told the good Douglas
> Who drew him soon into a privy place.
> Anderson told what stuff there was therein
> To Thom Dickson that was near of kin;
> Forty there are of men of mickle vail.
> Be they on foot they will you sore assail.
> If you happen the entry for to get
> On thy right hand a stalwart ax is set,
> Therewith you may defend you in a thrang,
> Be Douglas wise he hides not from you lang."

It was just daybreak, Anderson arranged the load and gave Dickson his clothes. The porter opened the castle gates and when the cart was between them, Dickson, with one blow, cut loose the piece of harness by which the horse was attached so that the load stuck fast, preventing the closing of the gates. He then killed the porter with his knife and seizing the axe that Anderson had told him of beckoned therewith to the ambush who rushed forward, slew the three wardens and took possession before the garrison were out of their beds.

The English soon, however, laid seige to the castle and Douglas led Dickson out through some postern or secret passage mounted on a fleet horse to warn Sir William Wallace.

> " Thom Dycson than was met with good Wallace
> Quhilk grantyt sone to reskew Douglace
> Dicson he said wait (*know*) thow thair multipli
> Three thousand men thair power mycht nocht be —"*

The English having notice of Wallace's approach raised the siege and retreated, but were overtaken and lost five hundred men.

For this and other services Dickson received the lands of Hisleside or Hazelside, about ten miles west of Douglas, where there is still a house bearing the name. There is scarcely a vestige of the old mansion remaining, but there are indications that it was a building of magnitude and strength.

Dickson must have done good service to his country for ten years later King Robert Bruce, about

---

* Two of these extracts are from the MS. of 1488. The second is from the edition of 1758 which is much modernized.

the year 1306, conveyed to Thomas filius Ricardi, the barony of Symundstun, now Symington, in the county of Lanark, and he was also created Hereditary Castellan or Governor of Douglas Castle. As such he resided in his own house except in case of war, when he left his house in charge of his dependents and himself took command of Castle Douglas.

Archdeacon Barbour's account of the return of Sir James to Douglasdale in 1307, is as follows:

" Now takis James his wiage
Towart Dowglas his heretage

*   *   *   *   *   *

And than a man wonnyt tharby
That was of freyndis weill mychty
And ryche of moble and of catcill
And had been to his fadyr leyll
And till himself in his youthed
He had done mony a thankful deid
Thom dicson wes his name perfey."

i. e.
" Now takes James his voyage
Towards Douglas his heritage

*   *   *   *   *   *

And then a man dwelt thereby
That was of friends very mighty
And rich of movables and cattle
And who had been loyal to his father
And to himself in his youth
He had done many a thankful deed
Thom Dicson was his name by my faith.
To him he sends and prayed him
That he would come to him at once
To speak privately to him
And he regardless of the danger went to him
And when he told him who he was

16

He wept for joy and for pity
And took him directly to his house
Where, in a chamber privately
He kept him and his company
That no one perceived it
Of meat and drink and other things they had plenty.
He wrought with so much subtilty
That all the loyal men of the country
That were dwelling there in his father's time
This good man made come one by one
And do their homage every one
And he himself first homage made."

Douglas then by Dickson's aid recaptured his castle of Douglas from the English, but according to Hume of Godscroft's History of the Family of Douglas (Edinburgh, 1648), being oppressed by the multitude of his enemies, Dickson was himself cut down and slain.

Barbour's account is as follows:

" Here Ja of dowglas slays them in the church.
The folk upon the Sunday
Held to St. Bride's church their way
And they that in the castle were
Issued out both less and more
And went forth their palms to bear
Except a cook and a porter.
Iames of Douglas of their coming
And what they were had notice
And sped him to the church in haste
But ere he came to it hastily
One of his friends cried ' Douglas, Douglas,'
Thomas Dicsone the nearest was
To them that were of the castle
Who were all within the chancel
And when he ' Douglas' so heard cry
He drew out his sword and fiercely
Rushed among them to and fro."

  *   *   *   *   *   *   *

According to tradition, although cut across the middle by an English sword he still continued his opposition until he fell lifeless, and this account, says Sir Walter Scott, is supported by a memorial of some authority — a tombstone still to be seen in the churchyard of St. Bride of Douglas, on which is sculptured a figure of Dickson, supporting with his hand his protruding entrails, and raising his sword with the other in the attitude of combat.

I regret to say, however, that Sir Walter was here at fault. In my visits to Scotland I had never passed through the town of Douglas, but in 1887, applied to the minister, the Rev. W. Smith, intending to have the monument photographed. To my surprise, however, neither he nor his sexton had ever heard of it. He then wrote to the Rev. Dr. Struthers of Prestonpans, a noted local antiquary, who remembered perfectly the churchyard as it was fifty-four years ago, and knew all the monuments, but said although there were a number of Dickson tombstones this was not among them. None of the oldest inhabitants, even those of the name, knew any thing of it. Mr. Smith then applied to the former grave digger, a very old man whose father had been grave digger before him, and offered him from me a reward if he would point it out. He said that Dickson was killed at the church door and buried before the door, but that there was no such monument. That he believed the former minister, the Rev. Dr. Stewart was mistaken in supposing there was one, and that he had always thought Sir Walter was misinformed or that he jotted down notes which he misunderstood. That Sir Walter visited the church but took down his notes in the hotel at Douglas from an old man named Haddon while the latter was eating the breakfast Sir Walter had given him, and that Sir Walter was very ill at the time and died not very long after.

His state of health was, therefore, probably also the cause that he overlooked the term " Dear Friend," by which Douglas addressed Dickson, as well as Barbour's statement, and called the lord of two manors a servant. Tytler also calls him a servant, while at the same time he says that Douglas lay concealed in Dickson's house and " Here night after night did his principal vassals assemble." A menial's house would hardly have been large enough or suitable for such a purpose.

THOMAS DICSON, Laird of Symonston and Hazelside, Hereditary Castellan of Douglas, was killed on Palm Sunday, March 19, 1307, aged sixty, and was succeeded by his eldest son.

THOMAS DICSON (II), whose successors the eldest branch at least, afterward took the name of Symonston, and with them therefore we have no more to do, except only to add that in 1335-6, Edward III, declared forfeited " 5 burgages,* now waste, in xvj s. viij d, at Sennewhare (*Sanquhar*) belonging to Thome son of Thome Dikeson."

---

* Lands held by a peculiar tenure.

The other sons of Dick de Keth or of Thomas Dicson (I), or of both, and perhaps also the younger sons of Symonston retained the patronymic, and from them the clan is derived.

The Dicksons were formerly one of the principal Border Clans of the East Marches, and according to Dr. Rogers (Traits and Stories of the Scottish People, London, 1867) were called

The Famous Dicksons,

and their daughters appear to have been likewise eminent, in their case we must suppose both for beauty and accomplishments, as the old rhyme says:

> " Boughtrig and Belchester
> Hatchetknows and Darnchester
> Leetholm and the Peel;
> If ye dinna get a wife in ane of thae places
> Ye'll ne'er do weel."

Buhtrig, Belchester, Leitholm and the Peel were Dickson baronies. Darnchester belonged at one time to the Trotters.

From Lanark the family soon removed to Peebles and Berwick. In the former county the name appears as early as 1338, and in Berwickshire in 1380, when Hugo Dekounson of Lathame is mentioned.

The Douglasses acquired lands in the county of Berwick in the reign of Robert I (1306–29) and a Keith was governor of Berwick-on-Tweed in 1333, which may account for the Dicksons settling there.

Chambers in his History of Peeblesshire says: " These Dikesons or Dyckisons (now modernized into Dickson), seem to have been an old and pretty numerous family in the district, for they turn up on all occasions in the burgh and other records."

Ade Dicson was Sheriff-Depute of Peeblesshire in 1338, and Ade Dekysoun was bailie or alderman of Peebles in 1400.

John Diksone was bailie in 1433, Thomas Dickesoun in 1444, William Dekysone in 1464, John Dikesoun in 1466 and Robert Diksone in 1480. John Dykkyson rendered the accounts of the bailies of Peebles in 1440.

Patrick Dikesone, bailie in 1482, had a grant under the great seal of £8, 3s. 4d. yearly for nineteen years to come for his services in capturing certain rebels to the king. Money was then many times more valuable than it is now. In the year 1300, an English Admiral of the Fleet only received two shillings per day, and as Hallam says an income of £10 or £20 was reckoned a competent estate for a gentleman, and a knight who possessed £150 per annum passed for extremely rich. And this was equal in command over commodities to £4000 at present. In 1391, a pension of twenty pounds a year was considered sufficient in Scotland for an ambassador, that sum having been settled for life upon Robert Grant, ancestor of the Grants of Grant. "He having been employed on various missions abroad," and about the same time that Bailie Dickson obtained his grant the following entry appears in the church warden's accounts of St. Margaret's, Westminster, A. D. 1476:

"Paid to Roger Fylpot, learned in the law, for his counsel giving, 3*s.* 8*d. with fourpence for his dinner.*" What would a modern barrister say were such a dole in our present currency offered him?

The bailies of Peebles were chosen from among the burgesses, and some value was attached even to the latter dignity, for in 1486, Allan Ewart furnished one hundred loads of stone for repairing the Tweed Bridge in requital for being constituted a burgess or freeman.

The position was not only an honorary one, but it conveyed several important privileges.

John Dickeson of Winkston was Provost of Peebles in 1572, —— Dikesoun in 1606, and John Dickiesonne in 1622. Matthew Dickson was Provost of Dumfries in 1582.

Noblemen often held this office. Among the Provosts of Dumfries were Lord Maxwell, Sir Roger Kirkpatrick and Lord Drumlanrig, and among the Provosts of Annan was the Earl of Annandale (afterward Marquess) who was succeeded in the office by his son Lord Johnstone.

Robert Dyckison of Hutcheonfield, county Peebles, had a charter from King Robert III (1390–1406) and John Dikeson of Smithfield in the same county, who was living in 1457, is the oldest recorded proprietor of that castle.

Henry Dikson was one of a party of five to whom a safe conduct was granted by Henry VI, King of England in 1426, to "George of Fallo, William of

Karylers, Patrick Kant, James Banbury and Henry
Dikson, Scotsmen, with six attendants, foot or horse,
baggage, ' ferdills,' etc., to come and to go between
England and other places at pleasure."

William Dicson was in 1445, a companion of Sir
James Stewart, Lord of Lorn, called the Black
Knight of Lorn, who married Jane Queen Dowager
of Scotland, for in that year a safe conduct was
granted by Henry VI, to " James Stewert lately
husband of the late Queen of Scotland, John Stewert
his son and William Dicson, Scots with twenty persons Scotchmen in their company."

This William Dicson was evidently a person of
consequence, for although there were twenty others
he is the only one mentioned by name in connection
with, *if not even as the equal of*, the step-father and
step-brother (Sir John Stewart, afterward Earl of
Athol) of the reigning King James the Second.

Patrick Diksone, Laird of Mersington, parish of
Eccles, county Berwick, was living at his bastel-house
and Will Diksone of the tower at his tower in Eccles
in 1479, when they were charged with treason along
with the Duke of Albany and others.

In 1544, the English army destroyed no less than
eleven or twelve places belonging to the clan, all of
which must have been of more or less importance to
have found a place in the report sent to the King of
England.

One year after this a bond was subscribed by the
Lords, Barons and Gentlemen of the March of

Teviotdale, obliging themselves to furnish one thousand horsemen to serve on the Border, and among the signers was John Diksone of Belchester.

In 1591, two bonds were signed by the principal Barons and Gentlemen of the East Marches pledging themselves to serve the King against Bothwell, and of the forty-one subscribers whose names have been preserved four were Dicksons.

Alexander Dickson, one of the above four, who was living in Edinburgh in the last decade of the sixteenth century appears to have been a prominent personage on friendly terms with Queen Elizabeth's ambassador in Scotland, and with the French ambassador in London, and to have been himself appointed Scotch ambassador to the Low Countries.

In Thorpe's State Papers there are two letters written by him and he is mentioned in five others, and as some of the extracts are curious I give them in full, premising that Bowes was the Queen's ambassador, Nicholson, Secretary to the English Embassy, and Sir Robert Cecil, English Secretary of State.

"Edinburgh, May 23, 1595. Anonymous to [Mr. Bowes]. The agents of the Catholic Lords very busy in their behalf. An evil spirit conjured from a young maid in Galloway. Angus holding on in the old fashion. An arrival from Paris. A casket of papers sent by Mr. Dickson."

"Edinburgh, July 9, 1595. Anonymous to [Mr. Bowes]. Mr. Dickson's uncle returned, but whether he brought any thing for his nephew he knows not."

17

"Edinburgh, July 15, 1595. George Nicholson to Mr. Bowes. Mr. Dickson will undertake the office requested of him. He wishes a passport to go through England. Argyle is sick and thought to be bewitched. McLane's willingness to serve against Tyrone. Lord Sanquhar will satisfy the Kirk. Disagreement between the King and Queen."

"Edinburgh, Aug. 9, 1595. Alexander Dicksone to Mr. Bowes. Thanks him for his loving mind and friendly endeavors, and professes a desire to do all good offices in return toward him and his sovereign. In reply to his request, he informs him that after he left the schools his genius and his youth inclined him mickle to the knowledge of the Affairs of the North, and that he gave himself to follow my Lord of Leicester, Sir Philip Sidney, and divers others the courtiers of the time; and he liked mickle for the same cause, to be acquainted with strangers and Ambassadors, and this was the ground of his resort to De L'Aubespine, and so he got all such discourses as he could, published or unpublished, as might advance his knowledge of the times he lived in. Describes the papers and books he possessed and offers to write to Mons. De L'Aubespine to prove his statement. Assures him that since he came to Scotland he never had any kind of commerce or intelligence by word or writing with any manner of men in England or any other of her Majesty's territories."

"Edinburgh, Sep. , 1595. Alexander Dickson to George Nicolson. Mr. Bowes to be informed of the arrival of Macwhinnie the priest who has come through England."

In 1596, a passport was given in Edinburgh by Mr. Bowes to Robert Dixon to go to London.

I continue the extracts —

"The Hague, Nov. 12–22, 1598. Mr. Andrew Hunter, Minister of the Evangel to the Scots Regiment in Holland to Sir Robert Cecill. The person who conveyed the letters to Scotland is expected again this summer; his name is John Young. Expediency of looking to him in England. Alexander Dixon expected from Scotland; his covert designs. Colonel Murray and Captain Hamilton's efforts to get him (Hunter) removed."

"Edinburgh, Dec. 16, 1598. George Nicolson to Sir Robert Cecill. The King and his Household receive the Communion; Angus and Errol do not; doubts about them. *Meeting of the Council.* The King's intercession with the Presbyters for the release of Lord Hume from excommunication. *An Embassy* to go to France. *Mr. Dixon to go to the Low Countries.* A foray by the Grahams."

This Alexander Dickson must have been a man of some importance when we find that a person deems it material to write to the English Ambassador solely to inform him of the arrival of Dickson's uncle. Then Dickson when offering to return Mr. Bowes' kindnesses writes as if he was assured that the Envoy knew that he (*Dickson*) had the power, if necessary, to be of service both to the Ambassador and his Sovereign, and lastly, although the French Embassy

was not yet composed, it was settled that Dickson
was to be Ambassador to Holland.

Sir Walter Scott in his Border Antiquities says that
"a little work called Monipenny's Chronicle, published
1597 and 1603, gives, among other particulars, a list of
the principal clans and surnames on the borders, not
landed, as well as the chief riders and men of name
among them." It commences " Bromfields (Chief,
Bromfield of Gordon Mains, or of that Ilk), Trotters
(Chief unknown), Diksons (Chief unknown)."

There were more than two editions of this work,
but I have not met with the one from which Sir
Walter made the extract. As before stated, however, the title should be "landed, and not landed,"
for the Records of the Privy Council are alone sufficient to prove that some of the Dicksons were
"Landit Men," and as regards the words "Chief
unknown," it would seem, on the contrary, that Buhtrig was the chief as in a Bond of 1573-4, Buhtrig,
Belchester and three others are styled the principals
and representatives for the surname of Dickson, and
in four other Bonds from 1563 to 1591, where they
also appear as a body Buhtrig always signs first.
That of August, 1591, was probably signed in the
order as they arrived, for near the head is Alexander
Diksoun, without local designation, and lower down
Buhtrig and Belchester.

Nisbet in his Heraldry (Edinburgh, 1722), says:
"There are several families of the name of Dickson
of good old standing in the shire of Berwick," and

names Dickson of Buhtrig, Dickson of Belchester, now the only old family of the name since Buhtrig has failed (*i. e.*, become extinct); Dickson of Newbigging next to Belchester; Dickson of Wester Binning and Sir Robert Dickson of Sornbegg, now designed of Inveresk, but the author here contradicts himself, and ·probably meant to say several families of "good standing," Belchester being then the only "old family. He did not, however, seem to be aware that Sir Robert claimed descent from the house of Buhtrig, and he overlooked the families of Hartrie and others.

From the year 1558, to the end of the last century fifteen of the clan were members of Parliament, as will be seen in the sequel, and the eldest son of the last laird of Belchester has represented an English constituency for several years.

Some of the clan left Scotland at an early date and became tenants of Furness Abbey, county Lancaster, one of whom, Sir Nicholas Dixon, Rector of Cheshunt, Prebendary of Howdon and Baron of the Exchequer, died in 1448; and from John Dixon of Furness Falls sprang Richard Dixon, Lord Bishop of Cork, A. D. 1570, and also Sir Richard Dixon who married the widow of the Lord Chancellor Eustace, and whose daughter Eliza (*ob.* 1745) married Sir Kildare Borrowes, 3d Baronet, who assumed the additional name of Dixon, and was ancestor of the present Sir Erasmus Dixon-Borrowes, Bart. John Dixon was also ancestor of the Dixons of Beeston, county York, now of Seaton Carew, county Durham.

It is of course impossible now to form any idea
of the number of the clan in feudal times, but in
1556, Buhtrig and Belchester attacked Douglas of
Kilspindy, Provost of Edinburgh, they having then
two hundred and eighty men.

These may have been a part only or perhaps the
whole of their own immediate followers, and if so
when those of the other chiefs, viz.: Hirdrig, Has-
singtonmaynes and Leitholm were united, as in the
case of a war with England, together with those of
the lesser branches as Newbigging, Westerbinning,
Newtown, Kennetsydehead, Kames, Loanhead, Peill,
Overmains, etc., in Berwick, Ormeston and others in
Peebles, the clan must have been able to muster a
considerable number of fighting men.

There is no county history of Berwick.   In Chambers' Peeblesshire and other recent works where our
name occurs it has been modernized, but where I
have obtained my information from older works or
records I have always given it as it appears.   When
the records are in Latin the Christian name only, as
a rule, is Latinized, and that I have translated.

The parish of Eccles in Berwickshire where many
of the clan were seated was anciently divided into
four quarters, viz.: (I) Lochton, Newtoun, Temp-
land, Fairnyrigg and Birghem.   (II) Mersingtoun,
Overplewland, Littlethank, Herdrig and Burnhouses.
(III) Lawrig, Buhtrig, Belchester, Newbigging, Anton's Hill, Peill, Stainerigg and Litem.   (IV) Kennetsydehead, Hassington, Nethermaynes, Whythouse,
Hardaikers, Stainfeeld and Dedriges.

CLAN DICKSON FAMILIES.

Although a Dickson of Leitholm, county Berwick, appears as early as 1380, only three generations removed from Thomas Dickson (I), still the houses of Buhtrig and Belchester seem always to have been recognized as the Chief, for Leitholm and others acknowledge their superiority in 1574, and Ormeston, the oldest of the Peeblesshire lairds, does the same in 1591, but the Marchmen often had their houses burnt and their writs destroyed, so that it is frequently impossible to trace their origin, especially as many of these old warriors disdained holding their lands by what they contemptuously called the "sheepskin" or "parchment" title, preferring to hold them by the sword.

A Hugh Dickson Esquire (*scutifer*) seems to have been connected with the shire of Berwick in 1431, if not earlier, for an inquest was held, dated Berwick, Sep. 2, 1408, regarding the right of Lady Margaret, relict of Sir John of Swynton, Knight, to her terce of his lands, and a transcript of the same was made at Perth, April 29, 1431, at the instance of "*providi viri* Hugh Dicson *scutiferi*," but to what house he

belonged does not appear.   He was probably, however, a relation or friend of her ladyship.

This roll therefore commences with Buhtrig and
Belchester, after which the families are ranked according to the oldest dates they are found in manuscript or printed records.

The first named, however, only appears as slain at
Flodden in 1513, and the second as receiving a Royal
Charter in 1539, but in 1591 a Belchester served heir
to his great-grandfather (*proavi*) John Diksone of
Belchester, who must have been living before 1539.

BUHTRIG.

ROBERT DIKSONE in Bouchtrig, county Berwick,
was one of the gentlemen who fell on the fatal field
of Flodden in 1513.*   He married Isobel Murray,
and had, with other issue, a son John who succeeded
him.

In 1552 Robert Diksoun in Bouchtrig and others
appeared before the Lords of the Privy Council and
signed an obligation to pay a sum of money to
Richard Maitland.   This was made by Robert Dixson
in the peill of Lethame, who probably headed the
list as the principal debtor, Robert Diksoun in Bouchtrig, Robert Diksone in the eist end of Lethame and
four others named Furde, Sanderson and two Red-
piths, and is signed "with our handis at the pen led
be the notar underwritten for vs becaus we culd
nocht writt."   The notary signed for all the seven.

---

* *Acta Dominorum Concilii.* Vol. **xxxiv**, fol. 136. 1 Mar., 1523.
Not published.

In 1557 Robert Diksoun of Bouchrig and John Diksoun of Belchester, as already shown, were charged with having, with a party of fourteen score (280 persons), pursued and slain Archibald Douglas of Kilspindy, Provost of Edinburgh, on August 8, 1556, and gave Alexander Lord Hume as surety that they would appear at the next Aire or Itinerant Court of Justice (Circuit Court) of Berwick.

Dicksoun of Buhtrig (no forename), Cuthbert Trotter in   , Hob Diksoun, Patrick Hume younger of Polwarth, Sir Robert Bell and others were accused Sep. 4, 1563, by Robert Hume of the Heuch, of having taken possession of his corn and goods, which it seems were claimed by Polwarth.

This and the preceding of A. D. 1557, in both of which legal documents he is called "of," proves that he held the lands then, but he appears to have forti- fied himself with a so-called "parchment" title soon after, for Robert Diksoun in Bouchtrig and Elizabeth McDowell, his wife, had a charter from the King and Queen of lands of Bouchtrig and lands in Lethame, Dec. 27, 1565, and six months after (8th July, 1566), the same were confirmed to Robert Diksoun, eldest son and heir of Robert Diksoun in Bouchrig.

The word "in" appears to be an error, for even if the Crown would not acknowledge his previous owner- ship the charter made him a landholder, and therefore "of," similar to the German "von."

Robert Dicksoun of Buchtrig, Robert Dicksoun, son of the Gudeman of Belchester, and Robert Dick-

18

soun of Hassington Manys, together with some fifty others (not Dicksons), signed a Band at Jedburgh Feb. 12, 1571, pledging themselves to rise against the King's enemies, etc., and to apprehend any rebels or thieves found within their borders.

Robert Dicksoun of Buchrig, John Dicksoun of Belchester, Alexander Dicksoun of Hirdrig and Robert Dicksoun in Eistand of Lethem, signed a Bond Jan. 19, 1573–74, obliging themselves as principals and representatives for the surname of Dicksoun that they shall behave themselves as dutiful and obedient subjects of the King and Warden, and that they shall keep good rule under the penalty of five thousand pounds.

In the Roll of 1590, as before stated, Buhtrig appears first among the landed men of his clan, as well as in Monipenny's List of 1597.

Alexander Dicksoun (by himself) and afterward Robert Dicksoun of Buchtrig, Andro Dicksoun of Belchester, and other border lairds, signed one of the bonds of August 6, 1591, pledging themselves to serve the King against Bothwell.

Robert Dicksoun of Buchtrig, Andro Dicksoun of Belchester, Robert Dicksoun of Ormestoun, Robert Dicksoun of Hassinden Manis and Alexander Dicksoun of Hirdrig signed a Caution agreeing to relieve the Lords Wardens of the Marches, Oct. 8, 1591.

In 1604, Walter Davidson was convicted and ordered to be hung for stealing horses, oxen, sheep, etc., from the lands of Pittilisheuch, belonging to

Dicksoun of Buchtrig and Sir John Cokburne, knyt. justice clerk. Although the stock belonged to them the land apparently then belonged to a Dickson alone, as a Robert Dickson of Pittilisheuch was taxed £8 in 1607.

In 1646, Robert Dicksoun of Buchtrig was a Commissioner of War. He married Agnes, daughter of Andrew Edmonston of that ilk, and died in 1647. His son, Robert Dicksone de Bughtrige served heir to his father in 1647. He was one of the Commissioners of War for Berwick, and was appointed Colonel of Horse and Foot in 1648. He was also an Advocate or Barrister, and as such was entitled Magister or Maister, and he was appointed Justice of the Peace in 1663. His arms were recorded in the Lyon Register as follows : " Mr. Robert Dickson Advocat descended of yᵉ familie of yᵉ Earle Marischall Bears azure three mollets argent on a chief or alse many pallets gules On ane helmet befitting his degree with a mantle gules doubled argent And torse of his collours is set for his crest a dexter hand grasping a sword in bend proper The Motto in ane Escroll, Fortes fortuna juvat."

Magister George Dicksone served heir to his brother in the lands of Buchtrigg, Lochrigs and Halfland, or Brewlands in Leitham in 1674. He was chosen Member of Parliament for New Galloway in 1678, but was said not to be qualified as he was not a residenter nor traffiquer in the burgh, but as he showed that he had succeeded as heir to his

brother Robert to some houses in the town, he was
approved of. In 1686, he was appointed Commis-
sioner of Supply (*i. e.*, for providing money for the
King). The Commissioners for this year were the
Duke of Gordoun, the Marquess of Douglas, the
Earle of Lauderdale, the Lord Ross, Sir William
Scot of Harden elder, Sir William Scot younger
thereof, the Laird of Wedderburn, Sir Alexander
Home of Rhentoun, John Home of Manderstoun,
Mr. George Dickson of Buchtrig, Alexander Home
of Linthill, Anthony Haige of Beamersyde, John
Home of Nynwells, John Home of Haliburton,
John Home of Broomhouse, James Dickson of Bel-
chester, Robert Dickson of Overmaynes, John Dick-
son of Newbigging, and ten others ; twenty-eight in
all, of whom four were Dicksons.

George Dickson of Buchtrig was witness to the
marriage contract of James Dickson of Belchester,
in 1689.

George Dickson of Buhtrig petitioned in 1698, to
be allowed to qualify as an Advocate, and although
he had been suspected as being unfavorable to the
government his petition was approved. It is not
improbable that there were two of the name of
George in succession, but this one appears to have
been the last of the family.

Buhtrig is still held by a clansman, having been
purchased by the father of the present Colonel
Archibald Dickson, R. A., of Chatto, Buhtrig and
Housebyres. It is a lonely place in the midst of

the hills. The old bastel house was demolished by the English in 1544, when the parish of Eccles was thoroughly wrecked, and although in the English reports it is sometimes said of a demolished tower that it had been destroyed in a previous raid and rebuilt, they had probably by this time learnt the power of gunpowder and ceased to rebuild such fortalices, trusting more, according to their ancient customs, to the security of the forests and mountains, agreeably to their old proverb that it was better to hear the chirp of the bird than the cheep of the mouse.

There are no ruins of stone and lime at Buhtrig, but a little to the south of the present farm-house the various mounds covered with grass clearly point out where at one time has been a building of considerable size, and this is borne out by the fact that various roads converge there. When the place was visited in 1887, a very old woman pointing to the spot said that it was the " Laird's House."

Between the farm-house and Greenhill there was formerly a hamlet or village, the foundations of which can be clearly traced, where the dependents of the laird probably dwelt, and that they were then numerous is evident from the many old places round the sides of the hills where they cultivated a patch of land, and from the walls which can still be traced which separated the cultivated part from the hill-tops where they grazed the black cattle. So long as cattle and horses were the principal stocking a number

of cottars were absolutely necessary to raise a sufficient quantity of winter produce for them.

In the immediate neighborhood of the "Laird's
House" is a place called the Moat, which is perhaps
one of the best preserved British strongholds in
existence. At the foot of the Moat have been buildings of stone and lime which were of course erected
long after the builders of the Moat had been forgotten. The materials of these buildings and of the
old bastel house were probably utilized for the building of the present farm-house and the numerous
walls, as the old castles generally served for quarries
for the country round.

BELCHESTER.

JOHN DIKSOUN de Belchester, county Berwick, and
Isobelle Hoppringle his wife, had a charter confirmed
by the King, Dec. 1, 1539. In 1591, however, a
John Diksone served heir to John Diksone de Belchester, his great-grandfather (*proavi*), who may
have been the father of the first-named John.

Johne Dikson of Belchest was one of the lords,
barons and gentlemen of the Merk (March) of
Teviotdale who, on the 4th Oct., 1545, subscribed a
Band obliging themselves to furnish one thousand
horsemen for the space of three months to remain
upon the Borders "to resist and Invaid our auld
enemys of Ingland."

Belchester also signed, next after Buhtrig, the
Bands of 1571, 1574 (as one of the principals) and

1591, was on the Roll of Clans in 1590 as a Landlord, and signed the Caution to relieve the Wardens in 1591.

John Diksoun was declared heir to his father, John Diksoun of Belchester, in 1632. James Dicksone of Belchester was Colonel of Horse and Foot and Commissioner of War for Berwick in 1648, and James Dickson was Commissioner of Supply in 1686, together among others with Haig of Bemerside, of whose family Thomas the Rhymer said six centuries ago :

> " Tide, tide, what'er betide
> There'll aye be Haigs in Bemersyde."

Three years later he married Hannah, daughter of Bemerside, and among the witnesses to the marriage contract were George Dickson of Buhtrig, advocate, and William Dickson, younger of Newbigging.

James Dickson of Belchester was out in the Rising of 1715, and fled to America — but he lived to return home.

The last Dickson of Belchester married Jane, daughter of General Sir Martin Hunter, G. C. M. G., G. C. H., of Medomsley, county Durham, and Anton's Hill, county Berwick. He sold the property about thirty years since and died leaving a son :

Major ALEXANDER G. DICKSON, M. P., late 16th Hussars, born 1834, married 1861, Charlotte Maria, daughter of the Rev., the Hon. William Eden and widow of Lord North. Major Dickson has sat in Parliament for Dover since 1865.

SEAT — Glenham Hall, Wickham Market,. county Suffolk.

LEITHOLM.

HUGO DEKONSOUN was paid £13.6 for the King's expenses while he was at Lathame, county Berwick ín 1380. As already stated this is the first mention of the name in the county.

John Dyksone in Lathame was appointed Tutor (*i. e.,* Trustee or Guardian) of Herdrig, which belonged to the late George Dyksone of Herdrig in 1517.

There appear then to have been two or more of the title for Robert Dixson in the peill of Lethame and Robert Diksone in the eist end of Lethame appeared before the Lords of the Council in 1552, and signed an Obligation together with Buhtrig, *q. v.*

Eumond Dikson in Leitholme, called Eumond of the Grene, with others, were at the horn * for the slaughter of Walter Fairley in Kelso in 1572.

Robert Dicksone in Eistand of Lethem was one of the principals of the Clan in 1574, and he or his successor appears among the Landed Men on the Clan Roll of 1590.

Alexander Dikson in Leithame gave an Obligation to Home of Stanerig in 1623, Robert Dickson, younger of Buchtrig being Cautioner and his brother James one of the witnesses.

The remains of Leitholm peel, razed in 1544, consisting of a fragment of the wall thirty-one feet long,

---

* Proclaimed outlaws or denounced as rebels for not appearing at Court when summoned.

about fifteen high and four feet thick, are still in existence.

ORMESTON.

ROBERT DYCKISON had a Charter of Hethonfields or Hutcheonfield, county Peebles, granted him by King Robert III (1390–1406). During the Regency of the Duke of Albany (1406–19) Malcom Fleming of Biggar gave to him a wadset of the lands of Oliver Castle, and in 1407, the estate of Ormistoun or Wormiston, county Peebles, with its peel, was conveyed to him. Ruecastle or Rowcastle, county Roxburgh, with its two strong towers also belonged to the family, but it was resigned by Thomas Dickinson of Ormestoun into the hands of King James IV (1488–1513). In 1491, Thomas Dikesoun de Or.' mestoun had the lands of Rauchen, Glenhigden and Glenchoen conveyed to him.

Thomas Dicsoun son and heir apparent of Thomas Dicsoun of Ormestoun, witnessed a deed in 1504. William Dickison held the estate in 1516, and John Dikesone de Ormestoun had a deed confirmed by the King in 1534.

In 1542, Dickson of Ormeston seems to have been called "of that Ilk," at least in his own county, for the Arms in Sir David Lindsay's manuscript are attributed to him.

Dikkesoun of Ormestoun was on the Roll of Clans in 1590 as a landed man. Robert Dickesoun of Ormestoun was the third in order who signed the Caution to relieve the Wardens in 1591 (*vide* Buhtrig).

John Dickesoun of Ormestoun was one of the subscribers to a general band against thieves, murderers and oppressors in 1602, and in 1628 Robert Dickson of Ormestoun was one of the mourners at the funeral of Lady Isobel Kerr, wife to William Douglas, Viscount of Drumlendrich.

The vault of the tower of Hutcheonfield is still in existence, as well as the ruins of the tower of Ormeston, which last was destroyed by the English army in 1544.

There was another Ormeston belonging to the Cockburns, which house was demolished in 1547.

MERSINGTON.

THOMAS DYKSOUN of Marsyntoun, county Berwick, A. D. 1455, was one of the witnesses to an acknowledgment by the Vicar of Swynton, of a gift of land by John of Swynton, dated at Swynton 16th July, 1455, "in the presence of honourable men, that is to say Alexander of Cokburn of Langton, Adam of Nesbit of that ilke, Robert of Blakater of that ilke, Thomas Dyksoun of Marsyntoun and Jhon Dyksoun his brother."

The same year he rebuilt the mills of Mersyntoune and Lettame. In early Scotch charters tenants are often obliged to use the mills of their landlords according to an old practice called thirlage, and pay multure accordingly. It was the same in England. At Castle Combe, county Somerset, as late as 1556, no tenants of the manor were to keep in their houses any mill called "quyrnez" ‚(querns), because they ought to grind at the lord's mill, under a forfeit of xx s.

Thomas Dicsoun of Mersintoune was on an inquest at Berwick-on-Tweed, 4th March, 1464, in a case concerning the lands of Cranschaws in the earldom of March, and Patrick Dicksone in Mersyntoun (perhaps a son of the laird) was summoned by King James III to attend an inquest concerning the same lands 16th March, 1476–7.

Patrick Diksone, the laird, was living at his bastel house in Mersington in 1479, when the Macer or officer of the court declared he had summoned "Pait diksone ye lard at his hous in mersingtoun david Jakson t Will dikson of ye tour at ye tour in eklis." They were charged with high treason in company with the Duke of Albany and others.

Thomas Dyksone in Mersintoun was on an inquest concerning the estates of Swynton at Dunse 6th Oct., 1500.

The bastel house was destroyed by the English in 1544.

SMITHFIELD.

JOHN DIKESON of Smithfield, county Peebles, was witness to a charter of Thomas Inglis of Manner, county Peebles, in 1457. He is the oldest recorded proprietor of the castle of Smithfield, which was destroyed about a century ago. John dikesone of Smethfeld, who signed an obligation in 1488, was owner of the lands of Melwelisland. William dikke-

sone was in 1494, son and heir of John in the lands
of Smithfeild and in a quarter of the lands of Edrigs-
toune.   John Dykison released the lands of Smeithfeild to his brother, Thomas Dikison, in 1500.

From the Dicksons the estate passed to the Hays,
by the marriage of the daughter and sole heiress of
John Dicksone to John, fourth Lord Hay of Yester,
who died 1557.

BYRTONANE.

JOHN DYKSONE of Byrtonane, county Berwick,
was living in 1484, when Sir John Swinton of that
ilk grants precept to his beloved friend (*dilecto*) John
Dyksone of Byrtonane to act for him.

BIRGHEM.

PATRICK DIKSON owned five husbandlands in
Byrgheame, county Berwick, in 1486.   A husband-
land in the Merse was anciently estimated at twenty-
six acres of land fit for the plough and scythe.

MAILINGSLAND.

JOHN DIKESON of Smeithfeild was owner of Melwelisland, county Peebles, in 1488.   In 1494, it
passed to his younger son Robert.   It seems then to
have been acquired by the Gladstones, one of whom,
John Gledstane of Coklaw, disposed of it to John
Dikeson of Winxton.   Richard Dikson of Mailweins-
land and his wife Janet, daughter and co-heiress of
Martin Wylie of Baumertoun, and Adam Dikson,
their son, were living in 1567, when Marion Wylie

conveyed lands to them. In 1580, Adam Dikson had a gift of the ward and nonentry* of these lands which were in the King's hands since the death of John Dikson of Mailingsland.

WINKSTON.

The Dicksons are said to have been in possession of Winkston, county Peebles, in 1489. In the Register of the Privy Seal is a precept for the confirmation of a charter granted by James Hamilton, son and heir of the deceased Margaret Mowat of Hanehous, to William Dikeson, burgess of Perth, of the lands of Winkeston, holding of the King 28th Oct., 1536. John Dikeson, son and heir apparent to William Dikeson, leased lands in Peebles in 1555.

JOHN DIKSOUN de Wingestoun was Member of Parliament for Peebles in 1568, and another of the family was Member of Parliament in 1612.

John Dickeson of Winkstoun and Aleson Udward his spouse had a gift of the nonentry of the lands of Cruikstoun in 1570.

John Dickeson of Winkstoun was Provost of Peebles, and was assassinated in 1572.

William Dickson, uncle of James Dickson of Winkestoun had a precept of the lands with tower, fortalice, etc., in 1581, on resignation of the said James.

A scion of this house went to Ireland and on the 4th March, 1646, Roberts, Ulster Herald, regis-

---

* The heir of the former possessor having failed to renew investiture with the superior.

tered to "John Dixon, Sergeant Major in Colonel Arthur Fox's Regiment of foot, descended from a very ancient and noble family of Dixon in the Marches of Scotland," the following ARMS— First and fourth, ar. a war-wolf * passant ppr. on a chief az. three mullets of the first. Second and third, a bull's head couped sa. langued gu. armed or. On a chief of the third an armory sword ppr. CREST — A pelican in her nest feeding her young. The quarterings show that one of the family married an heiress of the Turnbulls.

Part of the old fortalice now turned into a farm-house is still in existence. They had also a mansion in Edinburgh, in the Cowgate above the foot of Libberton's Wynd, where their Arms were to be seen in Nisbet's time (1724), cut in stone above the door.

HIRDRIG.

PATRICK DYKSONE of Heirdrig, county Berwick, was with Dyksoun of Mersington on an Inquest concerning the estate of John Swynton of that Ilk in 1500. George Dyksone of Herdrig died circa 1517, when John Dyksone of Leitholm was appointed Tutor of Herdrig.

Alexander Dicksoun of Herdrig subscribed the Band of 1573–74, as one of the principals for the surname of Dickson (*v.* Buhtrig). Alexander Dicksone of Hirdrig was on an Inquest for Robert Swynton in 1585–6.

---

* Werewolf, *i. e.*, manwolf or wolf with a man's head.

Hirdrig was on the Roll of Clans as a Landlord in 1590. Alexander Diksone of Heirdrig and others signed a Caution Sep. 6, 1591. He signed another Sep. 14, and likewise the Caution of October 8, 1591, to relieve the Wardens.

Although these Cautions were sometimes pledges to assist the Crown, they were also, in some cases, equivalent to our bonds to keep the peace.

James Dicksone de Herdrig was declared heir to his father Alexander Dicksone de Heardrig in 1617. John Dikson, younger of Herdrig, was witness to a Deed of Dickson of Kennetsydehead in 1623. Robert Diksoun de Heardrig was declared heir to his brother George Diksoun of Heardrig in 1626. Robert Dicksoun of Hirdrig was on an Inquest of John Swynton and others at Dunse, 20th Mar. 1628.

The fortalice of Hirdrig was destroyed by the English army in 1544.

TULYQUHENDLAW.

Mr. THOMAS DIKSON had a Charter of the lands of Tulyquhendlaw, county Forfar, confirmed by the King, 29th Nov. 1512.

HARTREE.

ROBERT DICKSON, born *circa* 1530, by his wife Anne, daughter of John Eccles of that ilk, county Dumfries, was father of John Dickson who married Agnes, daughter of John Boe, or Book, of Stane, county Lanark. His son, John Dickson, who acquired the lands of Kilbucho, county Peebles, in 1630, and those of Hartree in the same county in 1633, was nominated and appointed Colonel of Horse and Foot in 1643, Commissioner of War in 1644, and Member of Parliament for Sanquhar in 1645. In 1649, he was raised to the bench, when he took the title of Lord Hartrie. At his decease he gave Hartree to one of his sons and Kilbucho to the other, but the two estates became united again in the early part of this century.

In the seventeenth century, William Dickson of Kilbucho married Margaret, and John Dickson of Hartrie married her sister Anne, daughters of Sir William Murray of Stanhope, Bart., by his wife Janet, daughter of James Earl of Hartfield, and his wife Margaret, daughter of William, Earl of Queensberry. David Dickson of Hartrie married Helen, daughter of Sir Alexander Wedderburn of Blackness. Elizabeth, daughter of John Dickson of Hartrie, married Sir George Mackenzie, Lord Advocate of Scotland (ob. 1691), and their daughter Agnes (born 1663) married the first Earl of Bute.

John Dickson of Hartrie was Commissioner of Supply in 1704, and William Dickson of Kilbucho was so also the same year. John Dickson of Kilbucho was Member of Parliament for Peebles in 1747, and Brig. General William Dickson of Kilbucho, Lieut.-Governor of Cork, was Member of Parliament in 1802.

The last representative of the family, Alexander

Dickson of Hartree and Kilbucho, LL.D., Justice of the Peace, Deputy Lieutenant for the county of Peebles, and Professor of Botany in the University of Edinburgh, died suddenly while skating in 1888, and was succeeded by his brother, Archibald Dickson, Esq., of Edinburgh, M. D., born 1837, who is twelfth of Hartrie and eleventh of Kilbucho.

SEAT. Hartree House, Biggar.

BANCHRIE.

WIL DIKSONE in Banchrie, county Perth, was summoned on an assize in Perth in 1541, and they afterward became possessed of the lands, or part of them, as Jacob Dicksone, Portioner of Banchrie, died in 1642. His heir was William Dicksone, Senr., Burgess of Perth.

The term portioner, anciently parsenere, signified partner or co-heir.

HASSINGTON MAINS.

One of the strong houses razed in 1544.

ROBERT DICKSOUN of Hassington Manys, county Berwick, signed the Band of 1571, binding himself to rise against the King's enemies. Robert Dicksoun of the Manys in the Newtoun signed that of 1574, as one of the principals of the Clan. Robert Dicksoun of Hassingden Manis signed the Caution of 1591, to relieve the Lords Wardens of the Marches, and a Dikson of Hassington is in Monipenny's List of 1597.

20

In 1601, William Home of Ballycass was charged with the slaughter of the late Mr. Alexander Diksoune, son to the late Robert Diksoune, elder of Hassingtoune-Manis, committed the 21st day of April, 1597. Robert Dickson of Maynes was living 12th March, 1722, when Mr. George Dickson, Advocate, made a disposition to him.

Mains, manis or maynes signify demesne lands.

A small fragment of the old fortalice still remains, forming the gabel of a cottage.

NEWBIGGING.

This house was demolished by the English army in 1544.

WILLIAM DIKSOUN in Newbigging, county Berwick, is mentioned in a caution to Overmains and others, August 15, 1591, and a Dikson in Newbigging occurs in Monipenny's List of A. D. 1597. They appear to have been then tenants, but became afterward proprietors, as John Dickson of Newbigging served heir to his grandfather (*gudser*) John Dickson of Newbigging in 1654.

John Dickson of Newbigging was Commissioner of Supply in 1686, and in 1689, William Dickson younger of Newbigging was one of the witnesses to the marriage contract of Dickson of Belchester.

The Earl of Hertford says (Oct. 8, 1544), "burnt a Towne of New-byging and brought away from thence 100 shepe, 4 nolt, 4 naggs and 4 prisoners * * * and after came to Mersington." This proves that the Newbigging referred to was the Dickson barony, which was in the vicinity of Mersington. It is called a town, but in Scotland that word signifies not only a town as in England, but also a collection of houses, and sometimes even a single house.

NEWTON.

One of the fortified houses demolished in 1544.

ALEXANDER DIKSOUN of Newtoun, county Berwick, is mentioned in a Caution Aug. 5, 1691, to Dickson of Overmains, and Alexander Diksoun in Newtoun signed a Caution with Herdrig and others Sept. 15, 1691.

KENNETSIDEHEAD.

Another of the strongholds destroyed in 1544.

In 1612, John Diksone de Kennetsydehcidis, county Berwick, was the nearest relation on the part of his father Robert Diksoun, who was son and heir of the late Robert Diksoun, Jr., of Uvermanis, and in 1623, John Dikson of Kennetsydcheadis gave an obligation to Home of Slegden at Stanefauld, John Dikson younger of Herdrig being a witness.

STONEFAULDS.

Another of the peels ruined in 1544.

In a list of the Heritors of the Shire of Berwick, who attended or sent their servants to attend the Rendezvous on Fogo Moor in 1696, all of whom

were generally well mounted and armed with sword
or pistol, was John Dickson of Stonefaulds, who was
armed with a sword. This place was held by a
—— Dickson, Esq., as late as 1829.

INVERESK.

JOHN DICKSONE of Glasgow *temp.* Jac. iv (1567–
1625) purchased of Sir Matthew Stewart of Minto
the lands of Busby, county Lanark. He claimed
descent from the Buhtrig family and was father of
the celebrated Rev. Dr. David Dickson, Professor
of Divinity in the University of Edinburgh and
Moderator of the General Assembly when it was
broken up by order of Cromwell in 1653. He was
born 1583 and died 1663.

It is related that an English Merchant happened
to be in Scotland and having heard three of Scotland's worthies preach, describes them thus:—"First
I heard a sweet, majestic-looking man (Mr. Blair),
and he showed me the majesty of God. After him
I heard a little, fair man (Mr. Rutherford) and he
showed me the loveliness of Christ. And then I
heard a well-favored, old man, with a long beard
(Mr. Dickson) and that man showed me all my
heart."

Dr. Dickson's son, John Dickson of Busby, Member
of Parliament, was appointed Colonel or Commander
of Horse and Foot in 1649. He married Mary,
daughter of Sir Robert Montgomery of Skermerley,
by his first wife, the Lady Mary, daughter of Archi-

bald, Marquess of Argyle. His son, Archibald Dickson of Tourlands, county Ayr, was Commissioner of Supply for that shire in 1690. His son, Sir Robert Dickson, was created a Baronet in 1695, and took the title of Sornbeg from a barony he acquired in Ayrshire, and was afterward styled of Carberry and Inveresk. He married, in 1693, Helen, daughter of Sir John Colquhoun of Luss, Bart. by his wife Margaret, daughter and heiress of Sir Gideon Baillie of Lochend.

Sir Robert's Arms were recorded in the Lyon office before he was baronetted, as follows :—

"Captain Robert Dickson of Sornbeg and which Surname was originally Keith, Bears Argent three mollets gules on a chief of the second as many pales or. For his Crest within two branches of Laurel disposed in Orle an hart couchant guardant proper attyred or. The motto Cubo sed curo. Ext. 14th Sep. 1694."

This seems to have been *extracted* from some other record in 1694?

Sir Robert was one of the Founders of the Bank of Scotland in 1695, and was also one of the Barons in the Scotch Parliament who voted for the Union, being the first named on the list of thirty-seven Barons "Approvers." He died 1612, having had issue a daughter who married Patrick Grant, Lord Elchies, Judge of Session, and a son and successor Sir Robert Dickson of Carberry, Bart. who *d. s. p. m.* in 1760.

KAMES.

JOHN DIKSOUN in the Camis, county Berwick, was on an Assize in 1574. Patrick, son of John Dickson in the Camis, was witness to a Bond of Patrick Chirnside of East Nisbet, to John Dickson, son of the late Robert Dickson of Buhtrig, in 1592. John Diksoun in the Camys was party to a Bond in 1603 (*vide* Peill).

These may have been then younger sons or tenants, but were certainly freeholders soon after, as the successor, Patrick Dickson of Caimes, who died *circa* 1662, seems to have been a pretty large proprietor, but his son and heir apparent, John Dickson, signed a Renunciation from being served heir to his father 29th Jan. 1663, and the King ratifies, approves and confirms the Charter under His Majesty's great seal, granted to George Home of Caimes of the lands called Caimes, with the maner place, houses, bigings, yeards, orchyeards, parts, pendicles, anexis, conexis and pertinents thairof sumtyme possest and occupyed be wmq^{ll*} Patrick Dikson of Caimes. And of all and hail the lands called wester Caimes, with houses, biging, yeards, parts, pendicles and pertinents thairof whatsomever. With the bricks† of land underwritten, viz.: that brick lyand * * * with ane other brick of land lyand * * * Ane other brick * * * etc. To be holden of his Majestie and his Hienis successours, superiors thairof free of blensh

---

* The late.

† Portion.

for yearly payment of ane pennie scots at the feist of witsonday at the maner place of Caimes.

LOANHEAD.

JHONE DIKSONE called Jhone of the Loneheid, county Berwick, had a Deed confirmed by the King in 1574. Patrick Dicksoun, brother of Johnne Diksoun, called The Lonheid, is mentioned in a Caution in 1591 (*vide* Overmains).

This Patrick, younger of Loneheid, may have been the one who signed the Band agreeing to serve the King against Bothwell.

John Diksoun de Loneheid served heir to his father, Patrick Dicksoune in 1593, and Pat Diksone de Lonheid served heir to his father in the lands of Birghem, Newtoun de Birghem and Langbirghem in 1662.

PEILL.

This seems hardly a distinctive appellation in a country of peels, but it may have been either a large and imposing one, or a solitary one built when there were no others in the vicinity ; or perhaps it was the only tower among surrounding bastilles, and it is not unlikely that it is the very peel or tower mentioned in 1479, when the Macer summoned Patrick Diksone, Laird of Mersington, "at his (bastel) house," and also William Diksone *of the tower*, at *the* tower in Eccles, for it is here also called *the* tower *par excellence*.

The Laird of Peill, county Berwick, in 1590, is included among the Dicksons in the Roll of Ber-

wickshire Landlords, where they occur in the following order : Buhtrig, Belchester, Leitholm, Peill and
Herdrig, and either he was incorrectly styled "in"
in 1603, or the following applies to some younger
member of his family : "Edinburgh, June 21, 1603.
George Trotter of Prentonnan surety for Patrick
Diksoun in Belchester, William Diksoun in the
Grene, John Diksoun in the Camys, James Diksoun
in the Peill and James Diksoun in Quhitrig bound in
£1000 each to buy from Colonel Balfour such sort
of arms as they are bound to buy according to the
Act of Convention."

From this and other Cautions it would appear as
if the bondsman had to be of some other family?

There is a place on the Buhtrig estate still called
Peelneuk (Peel corner), showing that there was a
peel (unnamed?) there, probably the stronghold of
this family.   There are no ruins, but on the opposite
hill are remains of walls, etc.

OVERMAINS.

ROBERT DICKSOUN, elder of Over Manis, county
Berwick, Robert, John and Mr. Alexander Diksonis,
his sons, Alexander Diksoun of Newtoun, William
Diksoun in Newbigging, Patrick Diksoun, brother
of John Diksoun, called The Lonheid, Sir John Ed-
mondston of that Ilk, William Diksoun in Ednew,
Johnne Diksoun his brother, George Diksoun in
Harlaw and Johnne Diksoun his son were assured
in a Caution to the King, Aug. 5, 1591, by Hume of

Aytoun and others, "that they shall be harmless of them;" *i. e.*, Hume and his party agreed to keep the peace.

Robert Diksoun, Jr., of Overmanis was on an Assize in 1601. Robert diksoun of Overmaynes was Colonel of Horse and Foot in 1648, and Robert diksone of Overmaynes was Commissioner of War for Berwick and Commissioner of Supply in 1686.

Helena, Susanna and Lilias Dicksones were declared heiresses of their brother Robert Dickson of Overmaynes in 1694.

HARLAW.

GEORGE DIKSOUN in Harlaw, county Berwick, is mentioned in the Caution to Overmains in 1591, but they afterward became landlords, as George Diksoun of Harlaw is mentioned in 1609, and in a List of Heritors of the shire who attended a review (*vide* Stonefaulds) in 1691, was John Dickson of Harlaw, who was armed with a sword. Harlaw is a small place, however; only a farm steading, and the owner was, therefore, probably a so-called "bonnet laird."

SYDENHAM.

WILLIAM DIKSOUN in Ednew, county Roxburgh, was one of the parties mentioned in a Caution from Hume of Ayton, Aug. 5, 1591 (*vide* Overmains).

William Dikson in Ednem gave an obligation to John Dikson in Ednem, at Ednem in 1606.

John Dickson of Ednam and Sydenham, county Roxburgh, Member of Parliament for Selkirk and

21

Peebles, died 1771. His brother, Archibald Dickson. of Pontefract, county York, was father of Admiral William Dickson, whose son, Admiral Sir Alexander Dickson, Bart. (*cr.* 1802), was ancestor of the present Sir John Dickson-Poynder, 6th Bart., born 1866, of Sydenham, who assumed the additional name of Poynder in 1881.

SEAT — Sydenham, county Roxburgh and Hardingham, county Norfolk.

HADDINGTON.

ROBERT DICKSOUN was Portioner of the lands of the Abbey of Haddington, same county, before 1618, in which year his son, John Dickson, served heir to him. Patrick Dickson was Portioner of the same in 1636.

WHITSLAID.

JOHN DICKSON of Whitslaid, county Peebles, born 1629, a cadet of Kilbucho, was Commissioner of Excise for Peebles in 1661, and of Supply and of the Militia in 1689. He married Janet, daughter of Sir David Murray of Stanhope, by his wife Lilias, daughter of John, Earl of Wigton, and his wife Lilias, daughter of John, Earl of Montrose. His great-grandson, William Dickson, sold the estate of Whitside to his kinsman, William Dickson of Kilbucho, and settled in Jamaica.

WESTRAW.

JOHN DICKSONE of Westraw, county Berwick, was on an Inquest of Service of John Swinton of that Ilk in 1632.

STANE.

JAMES DICKSON, a cadet of Kilbucho, is said to have acquired the lands of Stane, county Lanark, from his kinsman John Boe or Book of Stane in 1640. In 1663, however, the King ratified a disposition made by William Lindesay in 1658, to James Dickson of Stane, with tour, houses, yeards, pertinents thereof, etc.

He was made Colonel of Horse and Foot in 1649. He married Janet Douglas, and secondly Margaret Edmonston, and had five sons and four daughters.

In 1663, William, Earl of Dumfries, gave a bond for 500 merks to James Dickson of Stane, writer (advocate) in Edinburgh, probably son of the preceding. This James had a son Alexander, who signed a bond in 1664.

LOCHARWOODS.

This was once entirely Dickson property, but was divided into Upper, Mid and Nether Locharwoods. The two latter have passed away.

THOMAS DICKSON of Nether Locharwoods, county Dumfries, born *circa* 1650, died May 5, 1717, leaving a son John, born 1682, died 1743, aged 61, leaving a son David, born 1727, died 1806, aged 79, having had issue (1) George, who died unmarried 1803, aged 25, (2) Richard Lothian, Major 1st Life Guards, who married Julia, daughter of Gen. Thomas Coxe, Foot Guards, and died in France in 1841. His eldest son, Lieut. Col. Lothian Sheffield, born 1806, was a Knight of the Order of St. Ferdinand of Spain.

JOHN DICKSON of Upper and Mid Locharwoods, born 1671, died 1751, aged 80, and was succeeded by his son, John Dickson of Upper Locharwoods, born 1719, died 1793, aged 74, and was succeeded by his son, William Dickson of Upper Locharwoods, born 1745, died 1827, aged 82, leaving a daughter and heiress who married —— Clark, Esq., and had issue a son, who assumed the additional name of Dickson, the present

WILLIAM CLARK DICKSON, Esq., of Upper Locharwoods, who married and has issue.

MONYBUIE.

THOMAS DICKSON of Locharwoods, county Dumfries, was born 1680. He was father of John Dickson of Conheath in the same county, Provost of Dumfries 1764–72. One of his sons, the Hon. William Dickson, M. L. C., settled in Canada, where he became Member of the Legislative Council, and was succeeded by his son, the Hon. Walter Dickson, M. L. C., who married and left issue.

From the Provost also sprang Walter Dickson, W. S., who married Margaret, daughter and coheiress of Thomas Goldie of Monybuie, Kircudbright, and was father of the present (1) John Dickson, W. S., of Monybuie, born 1817, married Eliza, daughter of Colonel A. Macleod, C. B. (2) Thomas Goldie, born 1819, J. P., married the Hon. Louisa Charlotte, daughter of 2d Viscount Sidmouth. (3) Walter George, M. D. and J. P. (4) James Gilchrist, married Jane Catherine, daughter of George H. Jackson, Esq., of Glenmore, county Waterford. (5) George, married Edith Mary, daughter of Miles Charles Seton, Esq., of Feskerby, Cornwall. (6) William, married Anne Stewart, daughter of Thomas Bruce, Esq., of Langlee, and (7) David Scott, married Hon. Frances Sophia, fourth daughter of 2d Viscount Sidmouth.

BARRETSTONE CASTLE (Ireland).

Sir KILDARE BORROWES of Barretstone Castle, county Kildare, third Baronet, married Eliza, daughter of Sir Richard Dixon, of a Scotch family (knighted in 1683, died 1709), by his wife, the widow of the Lord Chancellor Eustace. His son, Sir Walter Dixon-Borrowes, M. P., who inherited the estates of his maternal uncle, Robert Dixon, Esq., of Colverstown, county Kildare, and assumed the name of Dixon, was ancestor of the present Sir ERASMUS DIXON-BORROWES, 9th Baronet, High Sheriff, county Kildare, 1873.

WESTERHALL.

JOHN DICKSON of Westerhall, county Selkirk (?), was father of James Dickson of Westerhall, who married Maria Home, and was living in 1693.

WESTERBINNING.

Mr. ALEXANDER DICKSONE of Westerbinning, county Linlithgow(?), registered his Arms in the Lyon office between the years 1672 and 1694, as follows :

"Mr. Alexander Dicksone of Westerbinning descended of the familie of Buhtrig which was descended of the Earle Marshall Bears azur three mollets argent on a chief Or alse many pallets gules a bordur engrailed of ye third. On ane helmet befitting his degree with a mantle gules doubled argent and wreath of his collours is sett for his crest a man's heart volant proper with wings argent. The motto in an Escroll, Cœlum versus."

From the title Magister or Master he was probably an Advocate.

Patrick Dickson of Westbinnie was Commissioner of Supply for Linlithgow in 1695, and a contract of marriage between Patrick Dickson of Byning and Christian Dundas, only daughter of John Dundas of Manor, co. Perth, was signed at Edinburgh 26th Dec., 1696. John Dickson, only son of the deceased Patrick Dickson, of West-Bining, signed a Ratification in 1721, and the same John signed another deed at Edinburgh 4th Oct., 1725.

Nisbet, in 1722, mentions Mr. Alexander Dickson of Wester-Binning.

There are places called Bining both in Linlithgow and Haddington shires.

PERSILANDS.

MARY DICKSON of Kilbucho, county Peebles, born 1709, married in 1733 —— Muirhead of Persilands, county Lanark, who died leaving that estate to her. She died 1782, s. p., leaving it to her nephew Rev.

David Dickson of Edinburgh, ob. 1820, one of whose grandsons emigrated to the United States of America and settled in Indiana.

GOTHENBURG, SWEDEN.

JAMES DICKSON of Kelso, born *circa* A. D. 1715, believed to be a scion of the house of Westerbinning, was father of James Dickson, merchant, who settled in Montrose in 1780. His fourth son, James Dickson, born 1784, removed to Gothenburg, Sweden, where he died 1855. His son, Baron OSCAR DICKSON, Phil. Doct. of Gothenburg, born 1823, was ennobled in 1880 and created Baron of the Kingdom of Sweden in 1886. He married Countess von Rosen, daughter of Count Adolph E. von Rosen of Penningby, and has issue.

The baron has a signet ring which has been very long in the family on which is engraved the winged heart of the Westerbinning family together with their motto.

ALTON AND CHISHOLME.

ARCHIBALD DICKSON of Hassendeanburn and Horsley Hill, county Berwick, born 1718, was father of (1) Robert Dickson of Huntlaw and Hassendean, born 1742, who succeeded him ; (2) Archibald Dickson of Chatto, *q. v.*, born 1755, and others. One of his successors dying *s. p.* in 1846, was succeeded by his nephew, William Richardson of Alton, who assumed the additional name of Dickson, and died

1859, leaving a son, William Richardson Dickson of Alton, who died 1881, leaving two daughters, (1) Blanche Margaret Dickson of Alton and Chisholme, county Roxburgh, and (2) Jessie Mary Dickson.

CHATTO.

ARCHIBALD DICKSON, younger son of Archibald Dickson of Hassendeanburn (*vide* Alton and Chisholme), born 1755, married a daughter of Fisher of Housebyres, and was ancester of the present Colonel Archibald Dickson, R. A., of Chatto, Buhtrig and Housebyres, J. P. and D. L. for Roxburgh, and J. P. for Berwick, born 1829, married, 1880, Alice Florence, daughter of J. W. Seaburne-May, Esq.

BLACKBECK, ETC.

The Dicksons, formerly of Burton, county Lancaster, and of Blackbeck, same county, are of Scotch origin.

GEORGE FREDERICK DICKSON of Blackbeck, etc, had four sons, of whom the only survivor is the present Arthur Benson Dickson, Esq., of Blackbeck and Abbot's Reading. A Magistrate for the county. Born 1827.

CORSTORPHINE.

JOHN DICKSON, Esq. of Corstorphine, county Edinburgh, who died 1872, was father of John Heatly Dickson, Esq., of Corstorphine, Commissioner of Supply for Mid Lothian, born 1843, married, 1874, Anna, daughter of Sir William Collins.

In 1720, the lands and barony of Corstorphine belonged to Sir Robert Dickson, Bart.

WHITECROSS.

WILLIAM DICKSON, J. P. of Whitecross, county Berwick, was father of the present William Dickson, Esq., of Whitecross, a Magistrate for the county, who married, 1st, 1852, his cousin Dorothy, daughter of the Hon. Sir Henry Manisty, and secondly Frances, daughter of the late Francis George West, Esq., of Horsham Hall, Exeter, J. P. and D. L.

CLOCKBRIGGS.

DICKSON of Clockbriggs, county Forfar, Knight of the Order of the Legion of Honour, had a Grant of Arms in 1856.

WOOODVILLE.

DICKSON of Woodville, county Forfar. A branch of the Clockbriggs family as shown by their Arms.

PANBRIDE.

DICKSON of Panbride, county Forfar. A branch of the Clockbriggs family as proved ,by their Arms.

PEELWALLS.

JOHN DICKSON of Peelwalls, county Berwick, died leaving a daughter and heiress who married, in 1863, George Weir Cosens, Esq., eldest son of R. Cosens, Esq., of Kames, county Berwick. A Magistrate for the county and Captain in Her Majesty's 85th Light Infantry.

BARNHILL.

DAVID DICKSON, Esq., of Frogfield, county Kincardine, who died 1878, was father of the present

22

Patrick Dickson, Esq., of Barnhill in the same shire. Justice of the Peace for the county, married, 1856, Rosalie Isaline, daughter of M. François Favre of Geneva.

CLONLEHARDE.

SAMUEL AUCHMUTY DICKSON, Esq., of Clonleharde, county Limerick, had a Dickson arms confirmed to him by the English Herald's College, with a mark of Cadency.

STOCKTON-UPON-TEES (Town).

RICHARD DICKSON, Esq., of Stockton-upon-Tees, county Durham, is of Scotch origin. He is Lord of the Manor of Beverly-Watertown, county York.

Many landholders have undoubtedly passed into oblivion who have never been recorded, or whose records have been lost by the ravages so frequent on the Marches, while still others occur with but short notices of the names only, as the Dicksons of Qulentis, or Clontis, county Wigton, first mentioned A. D. 1471 ; of Cowiswark, 1574 ; of Roskuniefield, 1579 ; of Burnhouse, 1604, and of Quhitrig, 1607.

Besides these were the tenants, who were, as already shown, of the better class, and not sub-tenants or cottars ; as Dickson in Glenpoite, 1479 ; in Luthrie, 1480 ; in Rothuylt, 1480 ; in Le Kingis Barnis, 1480 ; in Railston, 1480 ; in Crawmond-regis, 1524 ; in Bothkennar, 1528 ; in Inglestoun, 1534 ; in Challachwrek, 1554 ; in Bonytoun, 1558 ; in Elistoun, 1575; in Bankheid, 1576; in Brochtoun, 1581; in Meginch, 1583; in Ancrum, 1590; in Quodquon, 1590; in Manerkirk, 1591; in Fairnyrig, 1591; in Esshiesteill, 1592; in Gourdis, 1592; in Mertoun, 1595; in Newtounheid, 1595; in Scotlandwell, 1595; in Preston, 1597; in the Grene, 1603; in Carphray, 1604; in Snawdoun, 1604; in Easthopes, 1604; in Airhouse, 1608; in Gordon, 1608; and in Fechane, 1609.

The dates given are when they first occur, but it is now impossible to show how long they had then been settled there, or how long they afterwards held the lands.

MEMBERS OF PARLIAMENT (ANCIENTLY CALLED COMMISSIONERS TO PARLIAMENT) TO END OF THE LAST CENTURY.

THE OLD SCOTTISH PARLIAMENT MET FOR THE LAST TIME IN 1707.

John Dickson of Winkston, for Peebles, A. D. 1558.

Patrick Dickson, for Peebles,(?) A. D. 1583.

John Dickson of Winkston, for Peebles, A. D. 1612.

John Dickson, for Sanquhar, A. D. 1645.

Andrew Dickson, for Inverkeithing, A. D. 1649.

John Dickson of Hartrie, for Peebles, A. D. 1649.

John Dickson of Busby, for Lanark, A. D. 1649.

David Dickson, for Forfar, A. D. 1661.

John Dickson, for New Galloway, A. D. 1661.

Robert Dickson, for New Galloway, A. D. 1663.

George Dickson of Buhtrig, for New Galloway, A. D. 1678.

Sir Robert Dickson of Inveresk, Bart., for Edinburgh, A. D. 1702.

John Dickson, Jr., of Kilbucho, for Peebles, A. D. 1747.

James Dickson of Broughton and Ednam, for Peebles and Selkirk, A. D. 1768.

Brig. General William Dickson of Kilbucho, Lieut.-Governor of Cork, A. D. 1802.

ARMS.

BELCHESTER. Az. three mullets ar. on a chief or, as many pallets gu. *Crest* — A dexter hand holding a sword in bend ppr. Motto — Fortes fortuna juvat.

BLACKBECK, etc. Quarterly, first and fourth az. three mullets ar. on a chief or, as many pallets gu. for DICKSON. Second and third, ar. on a chevron between three goat's heads erased sa. as many escallops of the field for Benson. *Crest* — First DICKSON. A dexter hand holding a sword in bend ppr. Second BENSON. A goat's head as in the Arms.

BUHTRIG. The same as afterwards borne by Belchester.

CHATTO, etc. Same Arms as Dickson of Huntlaw, with the bar engrailed. Same *Crest* and *Motto.*

CLOCKBRIGGS. Per fess az. and arg. in chief a mart. let or, between two mullets of the second, and in base a ship in full sail with sea, between a garb and thistle all ppr., on a chief of the third three pallets gu. On a canton the Decoration of the Imperial Order of the Legion of Honour. *Crest*—A dexter hand holding a sword in bend ppr. *Motto*—Fortes fortuna juvat.

CLONLEHARDE. Az. a crescent between three mullets ar. on a chief or, as many pallets gu. *Crest*—Out of battlements a naked arm embowed holding a sword all ppr. *Motto*—Fortes fortuna juvat.

GLENHAM HALL, *vide* Alexander G. Dickson (Major).

HUNTLAW Az. a bar or, between three mullets ar. On a chief of the second two pallets gu. *Crest*—A dexter hand holding a sword in bend ppr. *Motto*—Fortes fortuna juvat.

ILK. Of that, *vide* Ormiston.

INVERESK. Ar. three mullets gu. on a chief of the second as many pallets or. *Crest*—A hart couchant and guardant ppr. attired or, within two branches of laurel disposed orleways. *Motto*—Cubo sed curo.

NEWBIGGING. The same as Buhtrig, with additional figures for difference, as Nisbet says, but he does not blazon these marks of cadency.

ORMISTON. Ar. a wehr wolf sa., on a chief az. three mullets of the first. This coat of arms marked "Dikesoun of yat Ilk," and attributed to Ormeston, is emblazoned in the MS. of Sir David Lyndsay of the Mount, Lord Lyon King at Arms, A. D. 1542. A wehr wolf is a human-faced one, a heraldic animal, the French *loup-garou.*

PANBRIDE. The same as Clockbriggs within a bordure gu., but without the canton. Same *Crest* and *Motto.*

SMITHFIELD. Ar. three mullets, a chief gu. From a Funeral Escutcheon of the Hay Family.

SYDENHAM. Az. an anchor erect or, encircled with an oak wreath vert, between three mullets pierced of the second. On a chief of the last three pallets gu., the centre one surmounted by a mural crown ar. *Crest* — An armed arm embowed brandishing a falchion ppr. surmounted of a trident and spear in saltire or. *Motto* — Fortes fortuna juvat.

WESTERBINNING. Az. three mullets ar. on a chief, or, as many pallets gu., the whole within a bordure engrailed of the third. *Crest* — A man's heart ppr. winged ar. *Motto* — Cœlum versus.

WINKSTON. Ar. a were wolf passant ppr. on a chief az. three mullets of the first. *Crest* — A pelican in her piety.

A branch of this house as already mentioned quartered a bull's head sa. langued gu. armed or, on a chief of the third an armory sword ppr.

WOODVILLE. The same as Clockbriggs within a bordure ar. but without the canton. Same *Crest* and *Motto.*

Major ALEXANDER G. DICKSON, M. P., of Glenham Hall, co. Suffolk. The Arms of Belchester.

B. Homer Dixon, K. N. L., Toronto.

Ar. three mullets gu. on a chief or, as many pallets of the second. *Crest*—A hand holding a sword in bend ppr. *Motto*—Fortes fortuna juvat.

Charles Decksoune, A. D. 1481. A lion passant. On a chief a crescent between two mullets. "S. Charles Decksoune." Dalhousie Charters.

This seal of the year 1481, is from Laing's Descriptive Catalogue of Scottish Seals. Not being very legible a wehr wolf has probably been mistaken for a lion. "S." is the abbreviation of the Latin for "Seal of." The name generally accompanied the arms on old seals.

Sir Collingwood Dickson, G. C. B., V. C., Officer of the Order of the Legion of Honour, General in the Army. (Son of the late Admiral Sir Alexander Dickson, G. C. B., K. C. H. and A. D. C. to King William IV). Same *Arms* and *Motto* as Dickson of Sydenham, Bart. *Crest*—The same also, a crescent on the arm for difference.

Isabella Dyxcoun, wife of W. Nicolson. Three mullets. "S. Isabel Dyxcoun." Appended to Reversion of one husband-land in the town of Yester, A. D. 1527. Tweeddale Charters.

Sir Jeremiah Dickson, K. C. B., Major General. Ar. a chevron between three estoiles of six points wavy gu. on a chief of the last as many pallets or. *Crest*—On a mural crown or a stag couchant guardant ppr. attired or.

Baron Oscar Dickson, of Gothenburg. Quarterly, first and fourth ar. a rose gu. Second and third upon a bend an estoile ar. on an inescutcheon az. a man's heart ppr. winged ar. *Crest* — Over a baronial coronet, two coronetted helmets, on the first a man's heart as in the arms, and over the other a laurel wreath vert. *Motto* — Cœlum versus.

RICHARD DICKSON, Esq. Stocton-upon-Tees. Ar. three mullets gu. within a bordure engrailed az. bezantée, on a chief of the second three pallets or. *Crest* — On a mount vert between two branches of palm a buck lodged in front of a tree all ppr.

POSTSCRIPT.

As a rule it may be said that the sons, or at least the grandchildren of Scotchmen who settle in English-speaking countries, soon lose the language of their fathers, some even looking at it as one not to be proud of, but ours is not on a level with the different English provincial dialects as is generally considered, but as Mackay in his Dictionary of Lowland Scotch, says is, broadly speaking, classic old English, and as the London *Daily Telegraph* says, the terse and vigorous expressions of the Lowlanders are of older and purer extraction than many a word and phrase current with us to-day. "Neither the vernacular nor our literature would be the losers, perchance, if Dr. Mackay had the power, as doubtless he possesses the inclination, to weed our modern discourse of some of its thin, insipid colloquialisms, and fill their places by the best of the strong, harmonious language that gives local colouring to the pages of Scott and Hogg, Ramsay and Macneil. Who would not gladly see some of Burns' one-word sentences once more restored to use amongst us, and ousting some of the insipid and un-English jargon which weaken as well as deface the most widely-spoken, and, with fair play and wise conservatism, the most simple, mobile and powerful language in the whole world. English and Lowland Scotch were

23

originally the same, but the literary and social influences of the southern metropolis, after the transfer of the Royal Family of Stuart have favored the infusion of a Latin element into current English, which our kinsman were slow to adopt, and which we have taken with small or no advantage."

Another writer says : " The pure and classical language of Scotland must on no account be regarded as a provincial dialect any more than French was so regarded in the reign of HenryIV., or Italian in the time of the first Napoleon, or Greek under the Roman Empire.   Nor is it to be in any way considered as a corruption of the Saxon ; on the contrary it contains much of the old and genuine Saxon, with an intermixture from the Northern nations, as Danish and Norse, and some, though a small portion, from the Celtic," and Lord Brougham made these striking remarks, " There can be no doubt that the English language would greatly gain by being enriched with a number, both of words and phrases, or terms of expression now peculiar to the Scotch. It was by such a process that the Greek became the first of tongues as well written as spoken."

Let the reader peruse the following lines by the Rev. W. Mitchel, and it will be strange if their exquisite pathos does not make him think kindly of the tongue of old Scotland :

It's a bonnie, bonnie warl'
  That we're livin' in the noo,
An' bricht an' sunny is the lan'
  We aften traivel throo ;
But in vain we look for something,
  To which oor herts may cling,
For its beauty is as naething
  To the palace o' the King.

We like the gilded simmer,
  Wi' its merry, merry tread,
An' we sigh when hoary winter
  Lays its beauties wi' the dead ;
For though bonnie are the snaw-flakes,
  An' the down on winter's wing,
It's fine to ken it daurna touch
  The palace o' the King.

Then again, I've juist been thinkin,
  That when a'thing here's sae bricht,
The sun in a' its grandeur,
  An' the mune wi' quiverin' licht ;
The ocean i' the simmer,
  Or the woodland i' the spring,
What maun it be up yonner
  I' the palace o' the King !

It's here we hae oor trials,
  An' it's here that He prepares
A' His chosen for the raiment
  Which the ransomed sinner wears ;
An' it's here that He wad hear us
  'Mid oor tribulations sing,
" We'll trust oor God wha reigneth
  I' the palace o' the King."

Oh, it's honour heaped on honour
  That His courtiers should be ta'en
Frae the wand'rin' anes He died for
  I' this warl' o' sin an' pain ;
An' it's fu'est love and service
  That the Christian aye should bring
To the feet o' Him wha reigneth
  I' the palace o' the King.

The time for sawin' seed
    It is wearin', wearin' dune;
An' the time for winnin' souls
    Will be ower verra sune :
Then let us a' be active,
    If a fruitfu' sheaf we'd bring
To adorn the royal table
    I' the palace o' the King.

An' lat us trust Him better
    Than we've ever dune afore,
For the King will feed His servants
    Frae His ever bounteous store;
Let us keep a closer grip o' Him,
    For time is on the wing,
An' sune He'll come and tak' us
    Tae the palace o' the King.

Its iv'ry halls are bonnie
    Upon which the rainbows shine,
An' its Eden bowers are trellised
    Wi' a never-fadin' Vine :
An' the pearly gates o' Heaven
    Do a glorious radiance fling
On the starry floor that shimmers
    I' the palace o' the King.

Nae nicht shall be in Heaven,
    An' nae desolatin' sea,
An' nae tyrant hoofs shall trample
    I' the city o' the free;
There's an everlastin' daylicht,
    An' a never-fadin' spring,
Where the Lamb is a' the glory
    I' the palace o' the King.

We see oor fr'ens await us
    Ower yonder at His gate;
Then lat us a' be ready,
    For ye ken it's gettin' late;
Lat oor lamps be brichtly burnin';
    Lat us raise oor voice an' sing;
For sune we'll meet to pairt nae mair,
    I' the palace o' the King !

HOMER DIXON FAMILY,

WITH SOME NOTICES OF FAMILIES OF

COCKBURN, DALLAS, FRASER, HOWARD, HO-
MER, MAYNE, McKEIGE, PENNAZZI, ROBIN-
SON AND SMITH.

PREAMBLE,

SECOND PART.

As I am now over three score, and all my children are minors, I will commit to writing some account of my family, in case when I am gone some of my children should take an interest in the matter; a subject which, I regret to say, neither my father nor my grandfather cared about.

My grandfather, who was an only son, left home when a young man, and was thrice burned out, viz.: twice in the city of Westminster and once in Ostend; besides which his houses, both in Ostend and Flushing, were sacked by French troops. One of the fires in England occurred before the year 1786, when he and his wife were in the country, and it was at this time all his papers were lost, and he had had one or two family lawsuits before this date.

He married at the age of twenty-two, resided twenty years in Westminster, and then went to the Continent in 1788; and when his widow died in 1824, the silver plate, etc., and a box of papers was sent to us in Boston, but the latter was consigned to the cellar, and I remember cutting up some of the parchments to strengthen my kites, which almost

every boy played with in those days. Some years
after I overhauled the box again and found only a
few papers left, principally referring to General
Fraser.

When my grandfather removed to Ostend my
father was only seven years old. The first French
Revolution broke out four years after, in 1792, and
soon after the French invaded the Austrian Netherlands, and England and France were at war; and
from that time, *for nearly a quarter of a century*,
there were no mails nor hardly any communication
between the two countries, except by fishing boats
and smugglers, until 1815, when my grandparents
were not far from four score, and too old to think of
returning home. My father went to England in
1814, and remained about a year, principally in London, but all his relations of his own name were then
dead.

HENRY DICKSON, born *circa* A. D. 1712, married
and had issue (1) William, born in Dunblane, county
Perth, Scotland, in 1737, died young; (2) THOMAS,
of whom next, (3) Margaret, born 1740, died young;
(4) Margaret, born 1744. The only son,

THOMAS DICKSON or DIXON was born in Dunblane,
Nov. 6, 1739, and married at Inveraray, in 1762,
Elizabeth Mann (born 1738), daughter of Alexander
Mann or Mayne, of Renny, county Ross, by his wife
Katharine, daughter of the Hon. John Fraser, Master

of Lovat,* second son of Thomas Fraser, Lord
Lovat, Chief of the Clan Fraser.

MANN FAMILY. { Sir WALTER MAIGN, Knight, is the first
of this family on record. He had a
charter of lands in Aberdeenshire
in 1370, and from him descended families of the
name, written also Mayne, Mane, Main and Mann
who settled in the shires of Aberdeen, Forfar, Perth,
etc. Michaelis de Mane is mentioned in a Charter
of King Robert III (1390–1406). They may have
been of Norman origin from the province so called.

ALEXANDER K. MAIN of Renny or Rhynie (House),
county Ross, died in 1735, and was buried at Fearn
in the same county. He was father of

ALEXANDER MANN of Renny, born 1706, died 1802,
aged 96. He is called an Officer in the Army, and
was probably a subaltern in one of the Independent
Companies raised in 1730, as his wife's uncle, Simon
Lord Lovat, who was Lord Lieutenant of the county
of Inverness, was Captain of the first company (there
was no higher rank), and the privates were almost
all of them men of good families, many of whom had
joined as the carrying of arms had been prohibited,
and this service relieved them of that law.

---

* Master in the Highlands is the title of the eldest son of the
chief, or of the eldest brother if the chief has no son.

24

General Stewart of Garth, in his " Highlanders of Scotland," says five of these privates dined and slept at his father's house at Garth, and the following morning they rode off (although infantry) in their usual dress, a tartan jacket and truis, ornamented with gold lace embroidery, or twisted cords, as was the fashion of the time, while their servants carried their military clothing and firelocks.

There were six of these companies and a captaincy was considered equal to a lieutenant-colonelcy in the line. Each company wore the family tartan of its captain, but when regimented a dark tartan was given them, and they were then called the Black Watch, in distinction from the scarlet-coated troops of the line, who were known in the Highlands as the Red Soldiers. They were embodied in a regiment, against all law, in 1740, at which they were very indignant and mutinied, but order was soon restored, and they were sent to Flanders where they took part in the battle of Fontenoy. Mr. Mann was in this engagement but retired soon after. The family was not a Rosshire one. I think I heard that they came from Nairnshire.

FRASER FAMILY. GILBERT DE FRASER was living *temp.* Alexander I (1107–1124), and was ancestor of (I.) Sir Simon Fraser, the friend and companion of Wallace and Bruce, who

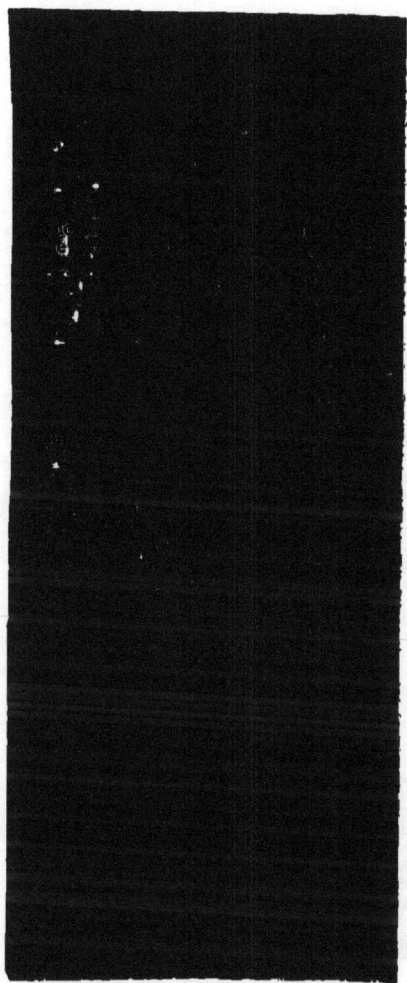

of whom were Frasers. The clan must
then have numbered probably eight or
nine thousand souls, for at the time General Fraser was without estate, money,
or influence, beyond that which flowed
from attachment to his family, person,
and name. In 1774 he was rewarded
with a free grant of his estate forfeited
to the Crown in 1746, and soon after
raised another regiment.

As regards the Norman French origin,
the Senachies anciently prided themselves in finding such origin, and even
called the Campbells "de Campo Bellos
or Beauchamps," equivalent to the English name Fairfield, while on the contrary the chiefs of Clan Diarmaid were
lords or petty Kings of Lochow, A.D.
420, and may have arrived there with
the first arrival of the Irish Gael in
Argyle in 258. A leader of the Gaels,
B.C. 279, was named Cambaul (Cam-
baules), and Caesar tells us that the
Gauls were accustomed to send their
children to England for their education, and it is not improbable, therefore,
that they were also intimate with Ireland; and as seven hundred years ago
seven of the family signed Ragman Roll
as Cambel, or Cambell, differing but one
letter from the present spelling, it is not
very improbable that they derive their
descent from the Gallic Chief of Cambaul.

Fabulists derive the Frasers either
from a Pierre Fraser, who they say
came to Scotland in 800, and whose son
was Thane of Man in 814, or from a
French noble, Julius de Berry, who in
the year 916 gave King Charles the
Simple such a delicious dish of strawberries that the King changed his name
to "de Fraise," and gave him fraises
or strawberries for arms. From him,
they say, descended the Frisell named
in the Roll of Battel Abbey. Unfortunately for those antiquaries, however,
coats of arms were not introduced until
more than two centuries later, or about
the time of the second Crusade, A.D.
.... before the days
.... or punning.
.... The Spanish
...... A castle
...... a gran...

...ain is called in Navarre una varra,
...d in the patois of the country, the u
...ing dropped, na varra, and the
...ings of Navarre bore a chain. In the
...me manner the Frasers probably
...lopted the fruit, which in the Norman
...rench or Romanıe, the Scotch court
...nguage of the time, was called fraisa.
The Frasers were, however, undoubt-
...ly Scotch ab origine, and Logan, and
...e believe correctly, considers the name
... be a corruption of the Gaelic Friosal,
...., Frith, a forest; (the th being quies-
...nt), and siol, a race—the Forest race
... clan, and in traditions they are
...lled Cearnaich na coille, or Warriors
... the woods.
In those days the nobles could not even
...ell, much less write their names. They
...re men of the sword, and used their
...als only, while the writing was gen-
...nlly done by the clerics or clergy, who
...re then but imperfect scholars, and
...uld not be expected to know the right
...elling of proper names, and in Rag-
...an Roll alone the name is written
...risell, Freshele, Fresar, de Frisle, Fris-
...e, and Fraser. Hugh Fraser, Lord
...vat, in an indenture of 1414, is called
...ressel, but probably when education be-
...me more common the present spelling
...came general, as agreeing better with
...ie arms. The clan name is Friosal, or
... Friosalaich, the Frasers.
The family must have been a most
...portant one in the time of Bruce, and
...ttled for ages in the south, for of the
...gners to the Roll, besides the Grand
...hamberlain and Bishop,* was another
...rd (dominus) and two knights. The
...ressel, and the two Sir Simons before
...entioned did not subscribe.
"Oscar" says the Fraser tartan is
...t an ancient one. Can he tell us when
...rtans were introduced, and which is
...e most ancient? He says, moreover,
...at Diarmaid, Con of the hundred bat-
...es, and others, are descended from the
...eat Clan Chattan (of which the Mac-
...hersons and not the Macintoshes were
...ie oldest branch), but that clan are de-
...ved from Germany, as I think I can
...rove if you should desire to have this
...rrespondence continued.—B. H. D.

was taken prisoner by the savage monarch Edward
I., and executed together with Wallace in 1306;
(II.) Sir Alexander Fraser, who married the Princess
Mary, sister of King Robert Bruce, and was killed
in 1332, and (III.) Simon Fraser of Inverness, first
Chief of the Clan Fraser, who took from him their
Gaelic name of MacShimi, or Sons of Simon. He
also was killed in battle in 1332. His grandson,
Hugh Fraser, was the first Lord Lovat. The seventh
Lord married a daughter and heiress of the Earl of
Athol, at whose death *s. p. m.*, King James VI.
offered the Earldom to the late Earl's nephew Simon
eighth Lord Lovat, and the King's Privy Councillor,
who however declined it "as a sinking of his own
title of Lord Lovat."

Simon Lord Lovat, decapitated in 1747, has been
painted by the Hanoverian party in the blackest
colors, but he was no worse than many of his con-
temporaries, English as well as Scotch.

Doublefacedness was by no means uncommon
among the ruling families, and with all his faults
Lovat was not to be contrasted with many whom the
country were delighted to honor.*

* As, for instance, John Churchill, of whom historians say that
he was an "almost indescribably profligate statesman; a lover of
pelf; as miserly as he was rapacious. He recoiled before no infa-
mous action when he had a purpose to serve. He was the favorite
of two Kings, both of whom he shamelessly betrayed. For years
he dabbled in army contracts, and meanly swindled the State by
drawing the pay of soldiers who were dead "—and he was created
Duke of Marlborough!

By the Jacobites, who judged him by his good
qualities, he was called " The Last of the Martyrs."
He is too often judged by his portrait, or rather
caricature of an old man of eighty, for Hogarth knew
what the mob wanted, and painted a picture that
would sell! Lovat's portrait by Le Clerc, painted
about the year 1715, shows him to have been then a
fine looking man. He preferred Prince Charley (the
gallant young Chevalier, as he was then; not the disappointed man of later years, who might almost have
been compared to the fourth George) to the house of
Hanover, and who can wonder. Not that the Stuart
was perfect; but what were the Georges? Any other
but a George would have pardoned an old man of four
score, or at least have left him to die a natural death
in prison. Lovat was so weak that he was brought
down from Scotland in a litter, and so feeble that two
men had to help him up to the scaffold.*

JOHN FRASER, master of Lovat, was born at Tan-
ich, Urray, county Ross, *circa* 1674. The record of
his marriage is lost, but my cousin, the late Capt.
Thomas Fraser of Balnain (who served during the
Peninsular War, but retired in 1815, and died in

---

* After the battle of Culloden, King George's second son, the
bloody Duke of Cumberland, also styled the Butcher, gave orders
to kill all the wounded; and not only were the fugitive Jacobites
slain without mercy, but the wounded were knocked on the head
like so many cattle, and this not in the heat of the battle, but in the
days that followed it. A number had huddled together into a barn,
and it was set on fire as the easiest way of getting rid of them, while
strings of helpless captives were fusiladed without mercy.

1860), believed that he married Elizabeth, daughter of Alexander Fraser of Balnain by his wife, a daughter of Fraser of Foyers.

The Hon. John Fraser was a consistent Jacobite to the last, and often resided in France. When in Scotland he bore assumed names, as John MacOmas (son of Thomas), John Dubh, or Dhu (dark haired or complexioned), and John Corsan, which was necessary as he was outlawed, for he was a faithful adherent of both the old and the young Chevalier. To check pursuit or to prevent suspicion, therefore, Lord Lovat always gave out that his brother John was dead.

The Frasers of Balnain were cadets of Erchitt, who in their turn were descended from the house of Farraline, the oldest offshoot of the house of Lovat.

The youngest son of above Alexander was Brig. General Simon Fraser younger of Balnain, who was killed at the battle of Saratoga in 1777. He was the officer who answered the challenge of the sentry at Quebec in French, and made him believe the troops who scaled the Heights of Abraham were the French *Regiment de la Reine.* They were suddenly challenged, but Fraser, who had been educated in France and spoke the language fluently, without losing his presence of mind exclaimed, "Hold your tongue, you fool, have you seen the English?" The sentry not being able in the dark to distinguish the uniforms and fearing to offend one of his own officers hesitated before demanding the countersign, and in that moment his musket was seized before he could fire

and give the alarm. A few years after at Saratoga
the American General perceiving that General Burgoyne (who was afterwards court-martialled) had lost
his head, called two of his best riflemen and said,
"You see that brave officer on the white horse. It
goes against my heart to do it, but you must pick
him off or we lose the battle." They succeeded,
and the Americans won the day, Fraser being the
second in command under Burgoyne.

———

Elizabeth Dixon, *née* Mann, was goddaughter of
John, fourth Duke of Argyle, and generally spoke of
him as her uncle, his sister having married her grand-
uncle Simon Lord Lovat in 1733. She told my
mother in Amsterdam that the Duke was very kind
to her, and that she had been a guest more than once
at Inveraray Castle. The Duke was Hereditary
Grand Master of the Household in Scotland, and
had some influence also in England, for there was a
vacant office at St. James', which he offered, but it
required residence at or near the Palace, and my
grandfather who did not like Court life, declined it.

My grandfather was a very kind-hearted man and
was robbed by his friends (!), and decided to go to
the continent where living was much cheaper. About
this time however (1786) my grandmother's uncle,
General Thomas Fraser, died in London. This was
Brig. General Thomas Fraser, Lieut.-Colonel of the

Royals and Lieut.-Governor of Chester, and previously Lieut.-Governor of the Island of St. Christopher, who died Nov. 5, 1786, a bachelor, aged 75,
and was buried in the Church of St. Martin's-in-the-
Fields. His tombstone is still in the crypt bearing
all the above titles, and at the foot the words, " E.
Dixon, *lapid. libens posuit.*"

During his last illness the General ordered his servant to send for his niece, my grandmother, as he
wished to give his Commission as Lieut.-Colonel
(then worth £4,000 or £5,000) to my father, for
whose benefit it could have been sold as it was usual
then to dispose of them, even on death beds. The
servant however said that our family had already
left the country, and no sooner was his master dead
than he ran off with about one thousand pounds in
money and the most valuable effects. Officers were
sent after him and recovered the gold watch (which
I still possess) and about £250 in money which was
all he had left. My grandparents were however
only out of town and were not aware of his death
until one of his brother officers, a General, came
down to offer Five thousand pounds for the Prize
money due the estate, as Gen. Fraser was one of
the commanding officers at the capture of St. Eus-
tatius in 1781, where the prize money was estimated
at Four millions, and his share, which had not been
distributed, was valued at Twenty thousand pounds.
The offer was of course refused. My grandmother
took out Letters of Administration Dec. 29, 1786,

soon after which sundry claimants appeared, and she had to oppose quite a number, and after gaining her case before the Courts of London and Edinburgh found she had expended nearly all she had received from the General's bankers, etc. At this time a new claimant appeared, and by bad advice of her proctors she gave up some papers which were afterwards withheld, and she was prevented from recovering the Prize money which was placed in Chancery.

When my father was in England in 1841, I persuaded him to look up this affair. He learnt then that early in the present century, I think he said in 1806, a certain Major Fraser of Newton laid claim to this sum, and as our family were then, as it were, *locked up* on the Continent, and ignorant of what was going on, as there were then no mails between England and the Continent, so that even if advertised they never heard of it, and there was, therefore, no one to oppose him, he succeeded in establishing his claim and the money was paid over to him.

About January, 1788, my grandparents went to Ostend, then a much more important place than at present. In 1792, the French Revolution broke out, and not long after the French invaded the Austrian Netherlands, now called Belgium. Mr. Dixon had invested some money in real estate which he could not sell, and was afraid to leave the country for fear it would be confiscated. He, however, raised as much money as he could and gave it to his wife who, with her son Thomas (my father), went to England, where she invested some of her money. Strange to say, I found a certificate for part of it between the leaves of an old book. It is a printed government certificate or receipt for £1,089 sterling, received of Mrs. Elizabeth Mann to pay for £1,800 consols, dated July 22, 1796. The receipt is in her maiden name, but Scotch women often retained their maiden name after marriage. It appears she bought consols at about sixty for one hundred. During the mutiny at the Nore, however, the year following, they went down to £45, the lowest point ever reached. Mrs. Dixon was afterward allowed to return to Ostend to join her husband.

The French had entered the city the day after she left, and Mr. Dixon was soon imprisoned and remained confined some weeks, until his Belgian friends obtained his liberty by giving bonds that he should not leave the country. On his release, he found his house had been taken possession of by General Beaufort with his wife and about fifteen officers and servants, and with difficulty obtained permission to occupy an upper room in his own house! Not long after the house caught fire and was entirely consumed, and moreover the French general claimed damages, conceiving the fault to have been in the chimney, for which he claimed that Mr. Dixon, as owner, was liable! And yet, as before stated, the general had quartered himself there, and of course without paying rent. The case was tried before the Tribunal of

25

Bruges, and Mr. Dixon gained it, but had to pay his own costs.

I have an official copy of the decree of court: "Citoyen Beaufort, Général de Division et Adelaide Barthelemy David son épouse *vs.* Citoyen Thomas Dixon," dated Bruges, 21 Vendemiaire l'an 6," *i. e.*, A. D. 1798.

There were no Monsieurs in those days. It was Citizen Dixon, and even the general was Citizen Beaufort.

Mr. Dixon was continually called upon to pay "emprunts forcés," or forced loans, and threatened with the guillotine if he refused. As a foreigner he was not spared, and was supposed as an Englishman to be rich. During these troublous times, he was again imprisoned, and was several times threatened with the guillotine.

About the year 1803, he removed to Flushing to be near his son Thomas, who was then engaged in business there, principally with the West Indies. He remained there until 1818, when he went to Amsterdam, where he died in 1824, aged nearly 85, and his widow died in 1826, aged 87. My father was then in Boston, and could not leave his wife and four young children for an indefinite period, especially as it was in the days of slow sailing vessels, when a voyage of two and even three months was not uncommon. His parents were, however, carefully attended to by their eldest son's widow. They had twelve children, all of whom pre-deceased them ex-

cepting only the youngest son. Nine died young.
The eldest son,

1. HENRY DIXON, born in Westminster in 1768,
was imprisoned two or three times by the French,
and his sufferings so undermined his constitution
that he died of consumption. He married Sarah
Watkinson and died in Ostend in 1802, leaving an
only son, Henry, who died cœlebs at Manilla, E. I.,
in 1823.

2. THOMAS, of whom next.

3. Elizabeth, born in Westminster in 1766, married
—— Eaton, of Craven St., Charing Cross (then a
fashionable West-end quarter), and died in 1790,
leaving an only daughter, Charlotte, born 1787, died
in Ostend, 1799, aged 12 years.

Thomas Dickson, who altered the spelling of his
name to Dixon, was succeeded by his only surviving
son

THOMAS DIXON, Knight of the Order of the Netherlands Lion and of the Order of the Lily, born
Westminster, Jan. 26, 1781. He accompanied his
parents to the Netherlands, and when about fifteen
years old a commission in the British Army was sent
to him by Sir Henry Dundas, afterwards Viscount
Melville, then Secretary of State, but it was inter-
cepted by the French Police and he was imprisoned
and sentence of death passed upon him, but a Law
had lately been passed that no executions should

take place in the Departments unless countersigned by the Minister of Police in Paris, and by the fortunate changes of Ministers of Police — three changes in about as many months — and the intercession of his father's friends, he was released upon bail that he should not leave the country.

In 1800, he left Ostend for Flushing, then like the former place a much more important city than now, and went into business.

While there another letter to him from England was seized by the Police. He had assisted a friend and fellow-countryman to escape, and this gentleman on his safe arrival in England unwisely wrote a letter of thanks, giving it to the captain of the smuggler who had taken him over. This skipper was like most of them, doubly a spy, taking pay both from English and French, and after undoubtedly first opening the letter to see that he himself was not implicated, he gave it to the French Police. Mr. Dixon was arrested and only escaped by bribing the Chief of Police with a purse of Fifty Napoleons or One thousand francs.

A few years after this he petitioned the British Government for reimbursement of certain losses, and among sundry certificates which he then procured was one which referred to the year 1804, and which I copy here :—

"This is to certify that in the year 1804, I commanded the British brig called the 'Eve,' of North Yarmouth was captured in the North Sea by the

French privateer the Admiral Bruix, and was conducted into Flushing, where, immediately on my
arrival, Mr. Thomas Dixon, merchant at Flushing,
rescued me from on board the privateer, conducted
me to his own house and kept me there in private
for three weeks, after which he conducted me on
board a Dutch schuit going to Rotterdam, which put
me on shore at Brouwershaven, according to the
directions of Mr. Dixon, with letters of recommen-
dation to his friends there, who procured me a passage over to England immediately.

"All which services Mr. Dixon did gratuitously, and
even furnished me with ten pounds in money, as
when Mr. Dixon rescued me out of the privateer all
I possessed was a few shillings, which I had previously communicated to Mr. Dixon. It is and was
well known that Mr. Dixon frequently assisted other
British masters in the same way, for which every
British subject ought to be acknowledging to him.

"Spencer Scott,
"Master of the Brig Liberty of this place."*

Between the years 1798 and 1807, he rescued from
different prisons between thirty and forty English
captains and seamen, and procured their passages
home at his own expense, and at great risk to himself had it been found out.

In 1808, he was appointed Magistrate of the city
of Flushing, and when King Louis (Bonaparte)

* Mr. Dixon's friends probably bribed some smuggler or fisher-
man to give Capt. Scott a passage to England.

visited the city he had the honor of a long conversa-
tion with him, and accompanied him on horseback
around the batteries, navy yard, etc.

When the Island of Walcheren was taken by the
English in 1809, he was ordered to continue in office
by the Earl of Chatham, Commander-in-Chief, and
when the English evacuated the city he was continued in office.

When the Emperor Napoleon visited Flushing in
May, 1810, he presented to him the keys of the city
and subsequently delivered an address as Chairman
of the Chamber of Commerce; but on the day following (May 12), was arrested by special order of
the Emperor, taken to Paris and confined as an
"Ôtage Hollandais" (Dutch Hostage) in the Prison
La Force, where he remained more than fifteen
months, three of which was in a dungeon, charged
with having served the English during the occupation of Walcheren, until by the unceasing efforts of
his friends van Royen, Bijleveld and Baron van
Doorn, *Deputés de la Hollande*, Bruys de Charly,
Deputy of the Department of the Saone and Loire;
Reverchon, old Member of the Council of Five Hundred, and Count Emmery, Senator, he was released
from prison and sent into exile at Macon in Burgundy, *sous caution et surveillance.* He was, moreover, ordered to sell all his property in Holland and
re-invest it in Burgundy, he being exiled there for
life, as legal copies of all the documents still in my
possession will prove.

The Deputy (or, as we should say, Member of Parliament) Bruys de Charly gave him letters to the Baron de Roujoux, Prefect of the Department of the Saone and Loire, and to others in Macon, and although my father did not say so in his memoirs (privately printed), still I think that Count Emmery must also have introduced him both to the Governor and to a brother Senator, as in a letter dated Paris, 28 Xbre, 1811, he says: "Dans votre Préfet, dans un de mes Collegues, vous avez la des protecteurs excellent."

The Prefect invited him to dine once a week regularly and gave him invitations to all his assemblies, and they were all very kind to him. He was an excellent whist-player and frequently took a hand at the Prefect's own table, so that he became quite intimate with him, and therefore passed the time not unpleasantly, except that as he was an exile, he had no passport and could not go beyond the city, for the country swarmed with gendarmes (military police) who would have demanded his passport, and not having the same he would have been arrested and again imprisoned.

At length after two and a half years, in January, 1814, the Baron sent for him at ten o'clock at night, and saying that he trusted to his honor, for if the Emperor heard of it he would be undone, told him that the German Army would soon be in Macon and all the exiles and Spanish officers, prisoners of war, were to be removed into the interior the next morning. That this was his only chance of escape, and from his friendly feelings towards him he could not bear to think of his being marched off by the gendarmes, and advised him to change his lodgings, promising not to order a particular search.

The next day, from his place of concealment, an attic of an unoccupied house, he beheld the prisoners marched off, and the following morning saw the Douaniers (officers of customs) running away. He then ventured out and met a detachment of Austrian Hussars, told the Colonel who he was, and in reply was informed that they were only an advanced guard with orders to retreat at the first resistance. The Colonel advised him to take lodgings opposite the bridge where he could give him warning. The next night the Colonel sent for him and they galloped off, pnrsued for some distance by a French mob, arriving the following morning at Bourg l'Ain, the headquarters, where the Colonel introduced him to General Count Bubna, Austrian Commander-in-Chief, who invited him to dinner, where he sat next to the General's aide-de-camp, Prince Leopold, afterwards King of the Belgians.

A few days later he arrived at Basle in Switzerland where he met an old acquaintance, the Chevalier de los Rios,* whom he had formerly known at The Hague, and who told him confidentially that the

---

* He was brother to the Duke of Fernan Nunez, and was afterwards Spanish Minister to the Congress of Vienna in 1815. I have two letters from him written at Vienna at that time.

King of France's brother, the Count d'Artois (afterwards King Charles the Tenth), was then in Basle
incognito under the name of Count Leu,* and upon
his saying he might give the Count some news from
Burgundy, the Chevalier asked permission to present
him, which was granted. He enjoyed the honor of
His Royal Highness' acquaintance about eleven
days, and was able to give him much useful information, and became quite intimate with him. The
Count wrote a Proclamation in the name of his
brother Louis XVIII., which my father got privately
printed and contrived to smuggle a few hundreds
into France. I have two copies of it. He then
left Basle and eight days after arrived at Nijmegen,
where he presented himself to the prince of Orange,
afterwards King William of the Netherlands.

Soon after he arrived at The Hague and passed
three months at the house of his friend van Royen,
then Minister of the Navy, and until the island of
Walcheren was evacuated by the French, when he
returned to Flushing, arriving there May 18, 1814,
and was reinstated in his office of Magistrate.

Shortly after the return of the Bourbons he received a letter from the Mayor of Macon, who with
three Deputies had waited upon King Louis to con-
gratulate him upon the Restoration,—informing him
that he had barely finished his address when the
King's brother said "Apropos, you had a Monsieur
Dixon in exile with you a long while. It was he who

---

* Louis Bonaparte afterwards assumed the very similar name of
Count de St. Leu.

26

first informed me of the good disposition of the Maconnais to the Bourbons, and it was in consequence of this assurance that I showed my favors to Macon in particular on my return. If you write Monsieur Dixon tell him from me that I remember him with affection."

Not long after the Baron de Vinck, a Dutch nobleman, was presented at the French Court, and the Count d'Artois asked him if he knew a Monsieur Dixon living in Holland, and upon his replying in the affirmative said if he would take charge of it he would send him a Decoration for his friend, and accordingly sent him the Patent (dated Paris, August 25, 1814) and Decoration of a Knight of the Order of the Lily.

About this time King William visited Flushing and my father accompanied him in a two hours' walk about the fortifications, and was listened to with interest as he had previously accompanied King Louis and the Emperor Napoleon on the same route. A dinner was given to the King and my father was seated directly opposite to H. M. who sat at the side of the table, in the middle. He then placed his resignation into the King's hands and soon after went to England where he remained about a year.*

---

*In 1839, King William I. granted me a private audience just before I was returning to Boston, having finished my education in Holland. After a few words (speaking Dutch) he said "But your father has lived here, has he not, I forget where?" "Yes, Sire (I replied) he was in Flushing when your Majesty first visited that city." "Yes (said the King) I remember, I dined with him there and he was then one of the Magistrates."

During his stay in London he petitioned the Lords of the Admiralty to refund the losses he had incurred at the time of his imprisonment, amounting to nearly £15,000 sterling, and especially because *he may be said to have saved the British fleet from destruction,* the suspicion of which was probably one of the reasons of his arrest. Had the French been able to prove it it would certainly have cost him his head.

The facts were that in 1809, a French officer's wife who had remained in Flushing and by some means had obtained the information, told my grandmother as a great secret that the French had prepared fire-ships in the Upper Scheldt and intended to burn the English fleet. My father did not return home until nearly ten o'clock P. M., when his mother told him. He immediately took a boat and went on board the ship of his friend, Captain Campbell, who without losing a moment took him to the Commander-in-Chief. The fleet were then lying in close order, but orders were immediately given to weigh anchors and prepare for fire-ships, and the French seeing this gave up the undertaking.

In 1814, Campbell, who was then a Rear Admiral, gave him the following Certificate, endorsed by Vice Admiral Otway:—

"These are to certify that, shortly after the surrender of the town of Flushing to H. M. Land and Sea Forces in 1809 (I, at the time, in command of H. M. Ship Audacious) I became acquainted with

Mr. Thomas Dixon, then merchant and acting as one of the magistrates of the said town of Flushing under H. M. Government, and found him on all occasions animated with the greatest zeal for the interest of H. M. Government and service, always furnishing H. M.'s officers with such private information as he could collect of the movements and plans of the enemy.

"On one occasion, I think to the best of my recollection, about the end of November in the above year, H. M. squadron and a number of transports then anchored at Flushing roadstead, he gave me for the information of the Commander-in-Chief certain and correct intelligence that the enemy were using the greatest exertions in preparing fire-craft and rafts in the Upper Scheldt, to send down the river for the annoyance, and if possible, the destruction of H. M. said squadron and transports, and this intelligence was afterwards proved to be entirely correct, and the arrangements made and orders given in consequence by the Commander-in-Chief had in my opinion (and indeed it was the general opinion) alone prevented the enemy from putting their plans in execution.

"Given under my hand, the 23rd Nov., 1814,

"D. Campbell.

"Rear Admiral."

Endorsed

"I recollect the circumstances as stated in Rear Admiral Campbell's certificate. The Admiral was then Captain of the Audacious and communicated to me, who then commanded H. M. ships in the Scheldt, in the absence of Sir Richard Strachan, the intelligence of the enemy's motives and intentions agreeably to information received from Mr. Thomas Dixon.

"Wm. A. Otway,

"Vice-Admiral."

Vice Admiral Otway also wrote the following official letter to J. W. Croker, Esq., Secretary of the Admiralty.

"Bath, 10th April 1815"

" Sir,—

" I request that you will lay before the Lords the Commissioners of the Admiralty, the enclosed letter from Rear Admiral Donald Campbell, with the certificate therein mentioned, stating some important service rendered to the public by Mr. Thomas Dixon of Flushing, about the month of November, 1809, at which time I commanded the ships in the Scheldt in consequence of the absence of the Commander-in-Chief Sir Richard Strachan.

" I have a perfect recollection of the circumstances as stated in Rear Admiral Donald Campbell's letter and certificate, who was then Captain of the Audacious, and I had no reason to doubt the authenticity of Mr. Dixon's intelligence; in justice to whom and at his particular request I make this statement for their Lordships to determine how far Mr. Dixon is entitled to any remuneration for the sufferings he

has, according to his narrative, sustained in conse-
quence of his attachment to the British Government.
··I have etc.,
"W. A. Otway,
."Vice Admiral."
"J. W. Croker, Esq."

The reply my father received was :
"That the Board of Admiralty cannot enter into
such claims as you have set forth unless founded on
documents forwarded officially to the Board at the
time when such services may have been rendered."

This was shamefully unjust, for the very documents accompanying these papers proved that my
father was imprisoned soon after this event and had
only just escaped from France, and even had he intended originally to have made any claim, it would
have been then impossible ; but he never dreamt of
doing so at the time, and it was only after the con-
fiscation of part of his property and his imprisonment
that he thought of it.

He also applied for the post of British Consul at
Antwerp, then worth £2,000 a year. General Sontag gave him the following letter :

"14 Buckingham St.,
"30th Nov., 1814.
"Sir,
"Lieut.-General Sontag being very dangerously ill,
has desired me to inform you, in reply to your letter

of 24th inst, that on hearing the circumstances stated in your letter, he perfectly recollected the very zealous and useful services rendered by you, and the applause you merited for the particular care and attention you afforded to the wounded English prisoners during the blockade and siege of Flushing, in furnishing them with all possible comforts.

"Lieut.-General Sontag hopes that this testimony given by me in his name may be found conducive towards the granting of your application for the British Consulship at Antwerp, which will afford him much pleasure.

"I have the honor to be, Sir,

"Your obedient and humble servant.

"David Ragay, Lt.-Col.

"Assist. to Lt.-General Sontag."

"Thomas Dixon, Esq."

Earl Bathurst, Acting Secretary of State, promised the Consulship to my father, but Earl Castelreagh, who was at the Congress of Vienna, gave it to the Hon. Mr. Annesley, son of the Earl of Annesley.

It will be observed that Admiral Campbell states the *certain* and *correct* intelligence was afterwards proved to be perfectly correct. My father said there were some three or four hundred sail in the harbor, great numbers of which would have been destroyed had it not been for his information.

From Parliamentary Papers (papers relating to the expedition to the Scheldt, Jan., 1810), it appears

that in July, 1809, the fleet consisted of one ship of
eighty guns, thirty-three of seventy-four (one of
which was the Audacious), three of sixty-four, twenty-
eight of from fifty to twenty guns, and ninety bombs,
gunboats, etc.   In all 155 sailing vessels of the navy.
On the 11th Oct. the transport tonnage then in the
Scheldt was 120 ships measuring 24,265 tons, and in
November nearly 20,000 tons of empty transports
had proceeded to Walcheren, a large proportion of
which reached their destination on the evening of
the 21st November.

One can hardly conceive what would have happened had such a number of vessels, lying quietly at
anchor and suspecting nothing, been surprised by a
fleet of fire-ships.

After the battle of Waterloo, Mr. Dixon returned
to Holland and joined the house of van Baggen,
Parker & Co., doing business principally with the
United States of America.   The style of the firm,
which was of very old standing, was changed to van
Baggen, Parker & Dixon.   The following year he
embarked for the United States to visit the corre-
spondents of the firm, traveled through the country
leisurely, and on his return to Boston to sail for
home, he became acquainted with and married Mary
B., daughter of Benjamin Perrott Homer, Esq., of
No. 37 Beacon St., May 26, 1818.

Duke Bernhard of Saxe Weimar, General in the Netherlands Army as
in-law of Queen Adelaide (wife of William IV), visited Boston
In his "Travels in North America, Philadelphia, 1828," he
"Mr. Dixon . . . introduced me to his wife and his father-in-law
This gentleman inhabits a large and handsome house on Beacon
and has two amiable daughters. I was much pleased with the
ments of his house, and indeed the houses and chambers in
larger and better adapted for convenience and ease than the En

HOMER
FAMILY.
} Thomas de Homere, Lord of the Manor of Homere, county Dorset, A. D. 1338, is believed to have been the founder of this family, especially as the name does not occur again there at that time, and in the same century a Homer settled at Sedgely, co. Stafford, and built the house of Ettingshall, which was occupied by the family until the last century, when it was sold by John Homer, who removed to another family property, Bromley Hall, in the same county, where he died in 1788. In 1626, Edward Homer erected a pew* in the old church of Sedgley, which was retained by the family until the church was taken down in 1829. The oaken seat of the pew is however still preserved and bears the following inscription:

"This : sete : setvp : at : the : proper : cost : and : charis : of : Edward Homer : anno : domni : 1626."

The grandson of this Edward was father of Captain John Homer, who emigrated to Boston, Mass., and was ancestor of Mary B. Homer, wife of Thomas Dixon, to whom we return.

On the 4th June Mr. and Mrs. Dixon sailed for England, remained a month in London and then went to Paris where they staid six weeks, and were most kindly received by the Royal Family, who only returned to the city the day before that on which

---

*At this time pews were generally confined to the lords of the manor or leading families.

they intended leaving. One of the Royal carriages was sent for them, and when introduced into the Presence Chamber the Count d'Artois met them at the door, embraced Mr. Dixon and kissed Mrs. Dixon, and then presented them to King Louis XVIII., who also kissed Mrs. Dixon and shook hands with Mr. Dixon. The Count then presented them to the Dukes and Du:chesses d'Angoulême and de Berri, by whom they were also most kindly received. The Count charged Mr. Dixon to apply to him if ever he could serve him, and when leaving told them to make what use they pleased of the Royal carriage. They accordingly took a drive in the Bois de Boulogne and meeting a Boston friend (Mr. Joseph Joy) gave him a seat. This gentleman as it was supposed (although it was headed "Letter from a lady") after his return home wrote an account of the presentation to a Boston paper, and I have still the slip which was cut out of the paper of April 20, 1819.

They then left Paris for Flushing to see their parents, passed a week at Ypenburg, van Royen's seat, and then went to Amsterdam where they remained about four years, when Mrs. Dixon, desiring to see her father, and Mr. Dixon wishing to make some business arrangements, they returned to Boston, intending to stay at most a very few years, but this was before the days of steam when it was not so trifling a matter to cross as it is now, and as the old couple died in Holland and Mrs. Dixon did not like to leave her father, who was a widower, they remained, until they finally determined to settle in Boston.

On the death of the Netherlands Consul in Boston in 1833, Mr. Dixon received the appointment. There was no Consul-General in the United States at that time.

Three or four years after the opening of steam navigation on the Atlantic they crossed again in 1841, and met many old friends.

At The Hague, which they visited two or three times, the King created Mr. Dixon Knight of the Order of the Netherlands Lion.

Baron van Hall was then Minister of Justice and his father was President of the High Court of Justice, and at a grand dinner given by his old friend van Royen, uncle to Baron van Hall, to which all the Cabinet were invited, my father was placed at the host's right hand, and the first toast given which was by the venerable President, was " The health of Mr. Dixon, who thirty years ago saved the life of my son, then in France as one of the *Garde du Corps* (Body Guard) of the Emperor Napoleon, and now meet him again for the second time as Minister of Justice of the Netherlands."

They returned to Boston, where he died at his house No. 1 Walnut St., Corner of Beacon St., Sep., 15, 1849, aged 68. His widow removed to Toronto on the occasion of her eldest son's marriage in 1858, and some years later was thrown from her carriage, the horses having run away, and died July 16, 1875, aged 83.

They had three sons, one of whom died unm. in Paris, and one dau., viz.:

1. BENJAMIN HOMER, of whom next
2. Fitz Eugene, born Amsterdam, 1821, married Philadelphia, 1849, Catherine Chew, daughter of the Hon. George M. Dallas, Vice-President of the United States of America, the first on record of which family was Sir William de Doleys, Knight, living in 1286. In 1442 John de Dolas held the barony of Cantray. From him sprang William Dallas, Laird of Cantray in 1630, ancestor in the third degree of Robert Dallas of Dallas Castle, Jamaica, grandfather of (1) Sir George Dallas, Bart. (2) Sir Robert Dallas, Lord Chief Justice, C. C. P. (3) Charlotte, who married Capt. the Hon. George A. Byron, father of George Anson, Lord Byron (the poet) — (4) the Hon. Alexander James Dallas, Secretary of the Treasury of the United States of America, *ob.* 1817, father of Vice-President Dallas, who filled also the offices of Envoy Extraordinary and Minister to the Court of the Czar and afterwards to the Court of St. James.

3. Harriette Elizabeth Mann, born Boston, 1825, married 1846, William Henry Boulton of Toronto, M. P. P., and Mayor of Toronto. Of the Boultons of Moulton, county Lincoln, England. He died 1874, *s. p.* She married secondly, Professor Goldwin Smith, D. C. L., Oxon. of the Grange, Toronto, son of Richard Prichard Smith, Esq., M. D., of Mortimer,

near Reading, England, by his wife, the daughter of
William Breton, Esq., and sister of Gen. Henry W.
Breton, Governor of Malta. Dr. Smith married
secondly, Katherine, daughter of Sir Nathaniel
Dukinfield, Bart. Of the Smiths of Hough, county
Chester, and anciently of Peel House, Farnworth,
county Lanc. Randle Holme, who visited Farnworth church in 1635, mentions a pre-Reformation
inscription on a broken painted glass window "Orate
pro Will Smyth" (Pray for William Smyth — not the
bishop however, for he was not buried there). Robert
Smith of Peel House was father of William, born
circa 1460, Lord Bishop of Lincoln, Chancellor of
Oxford and President of Wales (which had then a
Parliament of its own) who was one of the founders
of Brazenose College in 1509. Another son, Sir
Thomas, who removed to Cheshire, was one of the
executors of the bishop's will. He purchased Hough
in 1517. His grandson, Sir Thomas, Sheriff of
Cheshire, died 1614. One of his descendants was
cr. a Baronet in 1660. From another sprang Dr.
Smith above mentioned.

We now return to the eldest son of Thomas Dixon,
K. N. L., K. L.

BENJAMIN HOMER DIXON, K. N. L., Consul-General of the Netherlands in Canada, who was born in
Amsterdam in 1819. He was appointed Consul of
the Netherlands in Boston after his father's decease,
but resigned on his removal to Canada in 1858. He
was created Knight of the Order of the Netherlands

Lion by King William III, and in 1862, was appointed Consul-General.

He married firstly in Toronto, in 1858, Kate McGill, daughter of the Hon. Chief Justice Sir James B. Macaulay, C. B., who *d. s. p.* in 1865, and secondly, Nov. 29, 1866, Frances Caroline, daughter of William B. Heward, Esq., of Toronto, and Mary M. Cockburn, his wife. Frances C. Heward was born in 1838, and named after her two godmothers, her mother's aunt Frances, Countess dei Pennazzi, and her mother's friend, Lady (Caroline) Cunningham, both of whom were represented by proxies.

Frances C. Drain died Sep. 27. 1889. He m. thirdly Sep. 8, 1891, Emilie Maud Henrietta Caston, dau. of George Caston, Eq. Banker, of Balingston in, Eng. .—

HEWARD FAMILY. THOMAS HEWARD, Esq., of Friar Wingate, county Cumberland, England, had issue four sons and one daughter, viz.: (1) STEPHEN, of whom hereafter; (2) Thomas, married and died *s. p. m.;* (3) J. Elder, died *circa* 1872, leaving £80,000 in chancery. He had an only son who left home and has never been heard of. (4) Sir Simon, who was knighted in 1837 and died unmarried. The only daughter, Sophia, married Captain John O'Brien, Royal Navy. The eldest son, Lieut.-Colonel STEPHEN HEWARD, born 1777, emigrated to Canada and commanded the Queen's Rangers during the war of 1812. He married in Toronto, 1806, Mary, daughter of Christopher Robinson, Esq., M. P. P., and died 1828, aged 51. He was father of

WILLIAM BEVERLEY HEWARD, who married Mary M., daughter of James Cockburn, Esq., M. D., and had issue two daughters, (1) Frances Caroline, above-named, and (2) Mary Ann (Minnie), married James Henderson, Esq., of Toronto, barrister-at-law.

———

ROBINSON FAMILY. The Hon. CHRISTOPHER ROBINSON of Cleasby, county York, England (brother of the Rt. Rev. John Robinson, Lord Bishop of London and First Plenipotentiary of the celebrated Treaty of Utrecht in 1713), was appointed Governor of Virginia, where he died 1696. His descendant in the fourth degree, Christopher Robinson, M. P. P., had among other issue a son, the Hon. Chief Justice Sir John Beverley Robinson, Bart., C. B. (father of the late Lieut.-Governor of Ontario), and a daughter Mary, wife of Lieut.-Col. Stephen Heward.

———

COCKBURN FAMILY. ALEXANDER COCKBURN of that ilk, county Berwick, Scotland, was living *temp.* Robert Bruce, and numerous families claim descent from him, two of whom signed the Band of 1571, and two Lairds are on the Roll of Clans of 1590.

JAMES COCKBURN, M. D., Surgeon British Army, married Dorothea, daughter of Clotworthy McKeige,

Esq., and died at sea in 1819, leaving one daughter,
Mary Margaret, born in Quebec, in 1839, and married
William B. Heward.

McKEIGE } Clotworthy McKeige, Esq., of county
FAMILY. } Antrim, Ireland, and afterward of
Halifax, N. S., and Jamaica Plains
near Boston, Mass., nephew of Clotworthy, Earl of
Massareene,* and a relative of the Earl of Ellesmere,
married 1st, Isabel McDermot, by whom he had two
daughters, viz.:

1. Frances married Count Louis dei Pennazzi (son
of Count Louis de' Pennazzi and Princess Pallavicini
his wife) of Parma, Italy, Grand Cordon (now called
Grand Cross) of the Order of the Legion of Honour,
Knight of various Italian Orders and Lord Steward
of the Duke of Parma. The Countess died a widow
at her county seat Corte Maggiore in 1874. He died
1861, leaving (with a daughter Isabel, *detto* Ida, who
died unmarried in 1866, aged 18†) a son, the present
Count Louis de' Pennazzi, who married in 1862
Countess Albertine Ferrari (ob. 1876) and has issue.

2. Dorothea, married Dr. James Cockburn, before
mentioned.

---

* The Earl died 1805, *s. p.*, and the title became extinct by the
death of his brother *s. p. m.* The present Massareene is a Viscount
only.

† Although christened Isabel, the young Countess was always
called Ida.

He married secondly Eliza Church, by whom he had

1. Massareene William, who *d. s. p.* in Mexico, where he had a sugar plantation.
2. Ellesmere Edward, married Louise Spinola, and *d. s. p.*
3. Mary Louise, married Ernest B. Schneidler, British Consul at Cardenas, Cuba, and died a widow in 1875 leaving a son Charles, now in Hamburgh, and two daughters, viz.: [I.] Mina, married Louis B. C. Will, Grand Cross of the Order of Isabella the Catholic, Commander of the Order of the Royal Crown in Prussia, German Consul-General in Cuba, now residing in London, and [II.] Nellie, married Senor Don Ordonez del Campo, and resides in Havana.
4. Eliza, married Dr. H. Hoyt.
5. Augusta, died young.

Clotworthy McKeige, died in 1823, and his wife then took a house in Beacon street, Boston, but after a few years went to Parma to see her step-daughter and died there in 1837.

We return again to B. HOMER DIXON, K. N. L., who has issue

1. Thomas Fraser Homer, born 1871.
2. William Mayne Homer, born 1872.
3. Henry Eugene Homer, born 1874, and three daughters, viz.:

I. Mary Frances Homer.

28

II. Harriette Kate Macaulay Homer.
III. Ida Louise Homer.

Family of FITZ EUGENE DIXON (born 1821) of Philadelphia, who died in 1880, aged 58.

1. Alexander James Dallas, born 1850, m. Margaretta, daughter of Col. William Serjeant, United States Army, son of the Hon. James Serjeant, M. C., whose father, the Hon. J. D. Serjeant, was the first Attorney-General of Pennsylvania after the Revolution.

2. Thomas Fraser, born 1852, married Emma, daughter of Lieutenant Colonel C. J. Biddle, United States Army, and niece of Hon. Craig Biddle, Judge C. C. P., sons of Nicholas Biddle, President of the Bank of the United States.

3. George Dallas, born 1857, married Mary Frances Quincy, daughter of William H. Allen, Esq., LL. D., President of Girard College, by his wife Mary Quincy, granddaughter of the Hon. Samuel Quincy, Solicitor General of Massachusetts before the Revolutionary War.

4. Thomas Henry, born 1859, married Florence, daughter of William Henry Trotter, Esq., of Philadelphia, retired merchant and director of several banks, trust companies, etc. Of Scotch origin and descendant in the 7th degree from William Trotter, who settled first in Essex county, Delaware, but removed to Philadelphia in 1690 and died there in 1699.

5. William Boulton, born 1860.

And six daughters, viz.:

I. Sophia Dallas, married Francis John Alison, barrister, son of Robert Alison, M. D., grandson of the Rev. Francis Alison, D. D., of Donegal, Ireland, Vice Provost of the University of Pennsylvania.

II. Mary Homer, married Brigadier General Russell Thayer (graduate of West Point Military Academy), Commanding Second Brigade first division Pennsylvania Militia, son of the Hon. Martin R. Thayer, President Judge, C. C. P., of Philadelphia.

III. Catharine Eugenia, married Joseph Percy Keating, barrister, son of William V. Keating, M. D., whose grandfather, John Baron Keating, Knight of the Order of St. Louis (*ob.* 1856, aged 96) emigrated to the United States after the first French Revolution. He was grandson of Sir Geoffrey Keating, of Adare, county Limerick, who went to France after the siege of Limerick, and was created a Baron by the King of France.

IV. Harriette (Rita), married Arthur Emlen Newbold, barrister, son of John S. Newbold, Esq., of Philadelphia, a descendant of Godfred Newbold, of Newbold Abbey, county York, England, who emigrated to America in 1678, and settled at Newbold's Island, Delaware River, and afterward at Mt. Holly, N. J., where the homestead now is.

V. Susan Dallas, married Thomas Wilson Sharpless, son of Samuel J. Sharpless, Esq., of Philadelphia, a descendant of John Sharples of Sharples, county

Lanc, England, who emigrated to Pennsylvania in
1682, and received a grant from William Penn, of
1,000 acres of land in Chester county, a great part of
which is still owned by his descendants.

VI. Matilda Wilkins. She was named after her
aunt Matilda Dallas, wife of the Hon. William Wilkins, Secretary of the Navy of the United States
America, and Envoy Extraordinary and Minister
Plenipotentiary to the Court of Russia.

Catherine C. Dallas, wife of F. E. Dixon, died in
1878, æ 51.

Mr. Dallas Yorke, of Walmsgate Park, near Louth,
Linc., and Cadogan Place, who assumed the additional name of Yorke upon inheriting the estates of
his maternal uncle in 1856, is the present chief of
the Dallas Family. He was for some years Master
of the Southwold Hounds. He has one son, born
in 1875, and one daughter, who married His Grace
the Duke of Portland.

INDEX

OF BORDER AND OTHER SCOTCH SURNAMES.

ERRATA.

Page 17, line 13, omit "great."
Page 48, line 6, for "hoofs" read "houghs."
Page 82, line 10, after "Kirkmighel" add "(*Kirkpatrick ?*)."
Page 83, line 20, after "Laird of Cowhill" add "—— 91."
Page 91, line 10, after "Kirkmichael" add "(*Kirkpatrick ?*)."
Page 91, line 14, for "Kirks" read "Kirko."
Page 92, line 11, for "Blacadde" read "Blacadder."
Page 92, line 14, for "Horne" read "Home."

The following was accidentally omitted among "Clan Dickson Families:"

ANTON'S HILL.

John Dickson de Anton's Hill, co. Berwick, served heir to his grandfather (*avi*) John Dicksone de Anton's Hill in 1677. John Dickson of Anton's Hill was a writer in Edinburgh in 1712, when he and Janet Home, Lady Eccles, signed a joint bond which was only discharged in 1724. John Dickson of Anton's Hill was a Justice of the Peace in 1732. The last of this family, James Dickson of Anton's Hill, had an only daughter who m. the late General Sir Martin Hunter, G. C. M. G., G. C. H., of Medomsley, co. Durham.